CW00959126

Brassey's *History of Uniforms*

Brassey's *History of Uniforms*

World War One German Army

By Stephen Bull

Color plates by Christa Hook

Series editor Tim Newark

Brassey's

Copyright © 2000 Brassey's

All Rights Reserved. No part of this publication may be
reproduced, stored in a retrieval system or transmitted in any
form or by any means; electronic, electrostatic, magnetic
tape, mechanical, photocopying, recording or otherwise,
without permission in writing from the publishers.

First English Edition 2000

UK editorial offices: Brassey's, 9 Blenheim Court,
Brewery Road, London N7 9NT
UK orders: Littlehampton Books, 10-14 Eldon Way,
Lineside Estate, Littlehampton BN17 7HE

North American orders: Books International,
PO Box 960, Herndon, VA 20172, USA

A member of the Chrysalis Group plc

Stephen Bull has asserted his moral right to be identified as
the author of this work.

Library of Congress Cataloging in Publication Data available

British Library Cataloguing in Publication Data
A catalogue record for this book is available from the
British Library

ISBN 1 57488 278 3 Hardcover

Typeset by Hedgehog, Upton-upon-Severn, Worcestershire.

Printed and bound in Spain.

Contents

Introduction

In 1914, Germany was one of the youngest nations in the world, having existed as a country for only a little over 40 years. History had it that the first German Empire had been the medieval Holy Roman Empire, but in truth, though the German States were united in 1871, the constituent parts of the Hohenzollern Second Empire were divided by hundreds of years of separate development, dialect and even cuisine. More or less friendly rivalries between the states still existed, as did jealously guarded local priviledges, though her troops had all been marked with the stamp that was the Imperial German Army. Both politicians and outsiders were already identifying specific 'German' characteristics and stereotypes, but Germans often tended to categorise each other as industrious, lazy, civilised or uncivilised, depending on their state of origin and the observer's partizan point of view. As one military saying put it:

'A Pomeranian marches until he dies,
A Brandenburger marches until he drops,
A Saxon marches until he is tired,
A Rhinelander marches as long as he feels like it'.

Though a united Germany may have been new, her army, its organisation and uniforms were rooted in much older traditions. The core of the edifice was Prussia, a state in which paradoxically liberal, military and national traditions had coexisted for a more than a century. Many of the smaller states forces were more or less assimilated into the Prussian organisation, its War Ministry and numbered regimental systems, yet they retained their own special badges and honour titles and in many cases were formed into identifiable Divisions. The Bavarians continued to have not only distinctions of their own but a wholly separate

numbering system for their regiments. Whilst organised into Brigades and Divisions, which made up the 25 peacetime Corps, the building blocks of the German army were individual regiments of artillery, cavalry and infantry which retained their own identities.

A vital feature of the structure of the German army was the way in which existing regular line regiments were backed up by similarly numbered Reserve regiments, which consisted mainly of soldiers who had recently been demobilised, and these in their turn were reinforced by *Landwehr* units, and finally by the *Landsturm*. The standing army was filled mainly by conscripts. After two years, three in the case of cavalry and horse artillery, these men returned to their civil occupations, but were liable to serve in the reserve for four or five years, which in peacetime usually involved call out for two annual trainings. At the end of this period, men then went onto a reduced liability for *Landwehr* service lasting about 11 years. Finally, by the time an ex-serviceman was 39, he went onto the *Landsturm* which in peacetime entailed very little apart from appearing on the relevant list. Usually men joined the army for their conscript service at the age of 20, but additionally all Germans over the age of 17 were accounted liable for *Landsturm* service. This was essentially the system which had pertained in the Prussian army since the Wars of Liberation fought against Napoleon between 1813 and 1815.

So it was that although the peacetime German army numbered only about 800,000 in 1914, it proved possible to rapidly expand the ranks by calling up the reserve formations, plus the *Ersatz* or supplementary reserve. By Christmas 1914, the German army would number about five million and, despite huge losses, the seven million mark would be reached in 1917. By the end of the war, the original 51 'Active' combat divisions and 32 Reserve Divisions had been expanded to 212.

A sentry in the trenches wearing not only full trench armour with breast plate and three hanging plates, but the steel helmet fitted with the 'sniper' or brow plate. Notice also the standard issue Mauser G 98 rifle and the gas mask tin slung round the neck. BUNDES ARCHIV

Dress Uniforms 1900–1915

Infantry and Artillery

In 1914, the Imperial German army had ceremonial uniforms as splendid as any in the world. With minor variations the infantry of the line and the Guards wore a single breasted *Dunkelblau*, or 'dark blue' jacket, with scarlet collar and cuffs. This was worn with blue-black

A highly unusual photograph showing the Kaiser and King George V during a pre-war official visit. The Kaiser, left, is wearing the undress uniform of the British 1st (Royal) Dragoons of which he was Colonel in Chief from 1894 to 1914. King George returns the courtesy, appearing in the undress uniform of a Prussian Guard regiment.

trousers or *Hosen*, with a scarlet stripe down the outer seam of each leg. Senior regiments wore *Litzen* or decorative bars upon the collar. In summer (from the beginning of May to the end of September) the warm serge trousers were exchanged for a lighter type made of white linen. The dark trousers were often worn tucked inside the 1866 Model long marching boot, a practice which had been officially sanctioned since 1869, but there was also a black laced ankle boot which was worn with the summer trousers and in other orders of dress.

The usual dress headgear was the famous *Pickelhaube* or 'spiked helmet' of polished black leather; many of the myriad state and other variations of which are described below. On other less formal occasions, a blue cloth peaked forage cap with a scarlet band and piping was worn. This piece of headgear was a private purchase item, but there was also a visorless version of the cap on issue. Additionally, an eighteenth century-style mitre cap was retained for ceremonial wear by certain élite infantry units, namely the *1 Garde-Regiment zu Fuß*, the *Kaiser Alexander Garde-Grenadier-Regiment Nr 1* and the palace guard company. These *Grenadiermütze* or grenadier caps had a body of scarlet felt with white facings, and were fronted by a large regimental plate. The *1 Garde-Regiment zu Fuß* caps were further distinguished by a red and white pom pom and white metal chin scales and fittings; whilst the caps of the *Kaiser Alexander* regiment were decorated with a black and white pom pom and brass fittings. The palace guard wore the black and white pom pom and white metal fittings. Despite the antiquated appearance of the mitre cap the latest model had been sanctioned as recently as 1894.

The main distinguishing feature of the dark blue uniform jacket or *Waffenrock* was its shoulder straps which bore regimental numbers or cyphers, and varied with colour according to the Army Corps to which the unit belonged. Scarlet shoulder straps were worn by III, IV, XI, XIII and XV Corps; and white by I, II, IX,

Men of *Badisches Leib-Grenadier Regiment Nr 109* pose at the butts with their new G 98 rifles, July 1907. Clothing from every order of dress including the *Dunkelblau Waffenrock*, the fly fronted *Litewka* and fatigue garments are shown; the crown motif shoulder straps and collar and cuff *Litzen* of the Baden Leib-Grenadier regiment are clearly visible. The NCO in fatigue dress, right, demonstrates the 'charger loading' facility of the G 98. Several men wear the long bladed S 98 bayonet in black leather scabbard with bayonet knots in company colours. The shooting target, centre, depicts a prone figure and has been patched where struck by bullets. SB

and X Corps. Yellow was worn by the V, VI, XVI and XVII Corps; light blue by VII, VIII, XVIII and XX Corps; and light green by XXI Corps. Blue shoulder straps piped scarlet were worn by the XII, and XIX Saxon Corps. One Year volunteers also had a distinctive shoulder strap, edged by a twisted cord in the colours of their state. The main exception in terms of dress uniform in almost every respect were the Bavarian infantry, whose uniform was light blue with bright red facings, and scarlet shoulder straps in all of their three Corps.

The *Jäger* infantry battalions, or rifles, also wore a distinctive uniform of green with scarlet facings; the headgear being either a shako or a green peaked cap with a scarlet band and piping. For the majority of the *Jäger*, the shako was of black leather, but the Saxons and the 108th *Schützen* regiment had a felt shako reinforced with leather. The *Garde Schützen* were differentiated by black facings piped in scarlet. The *Jäger* legwear was again dark, almost black, trousers in winter; with white legwear for summer. Machine gun detachments were clad in a grey-green *Waffenrock*, with a shako of a similar colour reinforced with tan leather. Bavarian *Jäger* and machine-gunners were again exceptions with a light blue uniform faced in green.

What parts of the dress uniform were worn, and how, depended on the activity at hand. The four main orders of formal dress recognised in 1914 were *Paradeanzug; Wachtanzug; Ordonnanzanzug; and Ausgehanzug. Paradeanzug*, meaning literally 'parade' or 'review' costume, comprised the dress headgear with plumes if authorised for the unit; *Waffenrock* with orders and decorations, sidearms, belts, knots, rifle, pack and rolled greatcoat. All but musicians and standard bearers wore ammunition pouches. *Wachtanzug*, a stylised version of 'watch' or 'guard' dress was essentially the same but without the parade plumes or medals. In *Ordonnanzanzug*, or 'orderly' dress the pack and rifle and ammunition were

The uniforms of the Prussian Guard cavalry as depicted in the 1890s. Left to right: *Garde Kurassier* staff officer in court dress; Lieutenant *Garde du Corps* in 'gala' dress; Trooper *Garde du Corps* wearing the black cuirass; *Garde Ulanen*, officer Regiment Nr 1 and Trooper Regiment Nr 3; Guard Dragoon trumpeter; and *Leib-Husaren*, Lieutenant in court dress and staff trumpeter. From *Nachträge und Berichtigungen Zum Deutschen Reichsheer.*

dispensed with. The *Ausgehanzug*, the 'going out' or 'walking out' dress, featured the cap worn with the *Waffenrock* and trousers, belt, bayonet or sword, and knot.

In addition to the formal *Waffenrock* most units possessed two other uniform jackets. The *Litewka* was effectively an undress jacket of grey or blue cloth with concealed buttons: its name was derived from the word *Litauen* meaning smock. There was also a fatigue dress or *Drillichanzug*, of jacket and trousers, which was officially described as light grey, but was so light in tone that it was effectively off white. For the men the coat was short, somewhat shapeless, had a low stand up collar and six zinc buttons, and was worn without insignia; for non-commissioned officers the coat was more tailored and had a fitted waist seam and skirts. The *Drillichanzug* which was used extensively

for duties such as digging, drilling, carrying stores and food preparation soon became dirty but unlike the other types of dress was easily washed.

In winter or inclement weather, a grey greatcoat was worn by other ranks and a light grey greatcoat by officers, for mounted troops these coats were split up the back to make riding easier. The greatcoat was further differentiated by coloured collar patches, as for example red for infantry and *Jäger*; red with yellow lace for Guard *Jäger*; and black with yellow lace for Guard *Schützen*. *Litzen* and bars of lace to denote non-commissioned officers were also worn on the greatcoat collar patch. The 1901 model greatcoat was interesting in that it had a small hood attached under the collar, a feature dispensed with in the 1907 version.

Officers also had a choice of other over garments; amongst them were the undress top coat or *Überrock* which was double-breasted and looser fitting than the *Waffenrock*; the *Paletot* which was a light grey double-breasted coat worn for both service and parades; and the *Mantel mit Umhang*, a greatcoat with a cape. This last was not worn on parade, but off duty, or when mounted in the field.

Artillery dress uniforms were essentially similar to those of the infantry but there were a number of

Prussian Lancer uniforms in the 1890s. Left to right: One Year volunteer Regiment Nr 13; Lieutenant Regiment Nr 3 in parade dress; trumpeter Regiment Nr 11; NCO Regiment Nr 12; Major, Regiment Nr 5; Staff trumpeter Regiment Nr 15 in parade dress; Farrier, Regiment Nr 14; and Trooper in parade dress Regiment Nr 16. From *Nachträge und Berichtigungen Zum Deutschen Reichsheer.*

distinguishing features. Perhaps the most obvious was that they wore not a spiked helmet, but a leather helmet with a ball fitting on the top. Shoulder straps also usually bore a flaming grenade in addition to a regimental number, cuff details also varied.

Cavalry

Cavalry dress uniforms were, if anything, more eye catching than those of the other services, with a gaudy plethora of colour and a mass of distinctions which can only be summarised here. The heavy *Kürassiere* wore metal helmets and the *Garde du Corps* a black cuirass for ceremonial. The dress uniform of the *Kürassiere* was white, the various regiments being primarily distinguished by coloured facings thus:

Regiment	Facings
Garde du Corps	Poppy Red
Garde Kürassiere	Blue
Nr 1	Black
Nr 2	Crimson
Nr 3	Light Blue
Nr 4	Red
Nr 5	Rose Red
Nr 6	Russian Blue
Nr 7	Lemon Yellow
Nr 8	Light Green

The Saxon *Garde Reiter* had white distinctions and the Saxon carabiner, black. The light blue jackets of the Bavaraian *Schwere Reiter* had red facings.

Amongst the most dramatic dress uniforms were those of the hussars, the lineage of some units of which stretched back to the eighteenth century. The basic short jacket of the other ranks of the hussars was the 'Attila', decorated with five rows of white or yellow woollen frogging to the front and a line of lace extending down the back on either side. The cuffs were ornamented with knots. In the case of officers the braid was of either silver or gold, agreeing with the colour worn by the men. The cloth of the Attila could

Men of the Dresden-based *Sächsisches Feldartillerie-Regiment Nr 48*, c 1913. All but one are wearing the blue dress uniform with flaming grenade and numerals in red on the shoulder strap. Note also the *Kügelhelm* with ball mount and the Saxon star helmet plate. SB

be almost any colour of the rainbow, the hues of the 21 regiments being as follows,

Hussar Regiment	Attila Colour	Braid Colour
Life Guard	Bright Red	Yellow
1st Lieb	Black	White
2nd Lieb	Black	White
3rd	Bright Red	White
4th	Brown	Yellow
5th	Dark Red	White
6th	Dark green	Yellow
7th	Russian Blue	Yellow
8th	Dark Blue	White
9th	Cornflower Blue	Yellow
10th	Dark Green	Yellow
11th	Dark Green	White
12th	Cornflower Blue	White
13th	Cornflower Blue	White
14th	Dark Blue	White
15th	Dark Blue	White
16th	Cornflower Blue	White
17th	Black	Yellow
18th	Light Blue	Yellow
19th	Light Blue	White
20th	Field Grey	Field Grey

In many instances the spectacle was further enlivened by the fact that officers' jackets were lighter in shade than those of the other ranks. In the 5th *Fürst Blücher von Wahlstatt* hussars for example the Attila of the officers was more pink than red. In the 4th *von Schill* (Silesian) hussars, the officers' jacket was a reddish brown rather than the deep brown worn by the men. It was also the case that in certain orders of dress, officers were allowed the use of an undress tunic or 'Interim Attila': this garment was somewhat simpler than the full dress Attila lacking the rank lace on its collar and cuffs. Generally it was in the same colour as the Attila but the Life Guard hussars and the 3rd and 5th wore the Interim Attila in dark blue. Officers and other ranks were also permitted the use of a *Litewka* or grey working jacket. For other ranks, this was single-breasted and fly fronted, and for officers double-breasted with two rows of six buttons. Officers wore collar tabs, and other ranks collar patches, often in the colour of the Attila but as usual there were

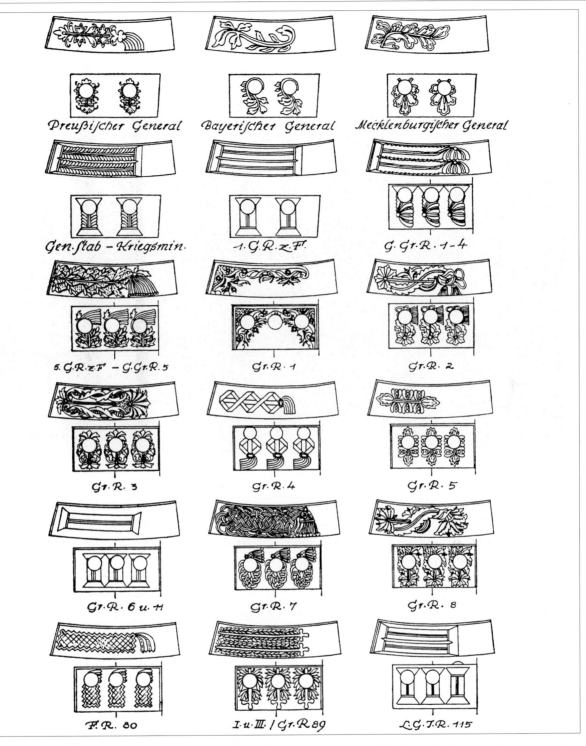

Preußischer General   Bayerischer General   Mecklenburgischer General

Gen.Stab – Kriegsmin.   1.G.R.z.F.   G.Gr.R.1-4

5.G.R.z.F. – G.Gr.R.5   Gr.R.1   Gr.R.2

Gr.R.3   Gr.R.4   Gr.R.5

Gr.R.6 u.11   Gr.R.7   Gr.R.8

F.R.80   I.u.III./Gr.R.89   L.G.I.R.115

The distinctive types of lace and *Litzen* for various states and regiments. Notice in particular the difference between the collar lace of the generals of different states: Prussian, Bavarian and Mecklenburger.

variations. The main exceptions were the collar patches of the Life Guard hussars which had double yellow Guard *Litzen* superimposed upon them; the 10th which had deep pink patches; the 15th which had yellow patches; the 18th which had red; and the 19th crimson.

Not all regiments of hussars were entitled to wear the *Pelz* or pelisse, the over jacket trimmed with fur, as this had been abolished in 1853, and only certain units had been reissued with it since – often as a gift from their colonel in chief. In all cases the fur trimmings for officers were light grey, but the colour of the cloth and colour of the fur for other ranks varied from regiment to regiment in the nine units that wore it:

Hussar Regiment	Pelz Colour	Other Ranks Fur Colour	Cuff type
Life Guard	Dark Blue	Black	Brandenburg
1st Leib	Black	Light Grey	Pointed

Prussian Dragoons, 1890s. Left to right: Regiment Nr 1, Lieutenant Colonel in parade dress; Regiment Nr 14, Adjutant; Regiment Nr 16 Captain in the uniform of a personal Adjutant to a Prince; Lieutenant Regiment Nr 9; NCO Regiment Nr 12; Regiment Nr 4, trumpeter in parade dress; NCO in fatigue dress Regiment Nr 2; One Year volunteer Regiment Nr 3. *From Nachträge und Berichtigungen Zum Deutschen Reichsheer.*

2nd Leib	Black	Light Grey	Pointed
3rd	Dark Blue	Light Grey	Brandenburg
8th	Dark Blue	White	Pointed
12th	Cornflower Blue	White	Pointed
13th	Cornflower Blue	Light Grey	Pointed
15th	Dark Blue	Black	Brandenburg
16th	Cornflower Blue	White	Pointed

Hussars generally wore either blue black riding breeches or *Reithosen*, or during summer months white linen trousers. The exceptions to this general rule were the 18th and 19th regiments who wore light blue breeches and the 20th who wore field grey. The stripe down the outside of the legs of the breeches was yellow, white, gold or silver, depending on the lace colour of the regiment and whether the wearer was an officer or other rank. Additionally, general officers who wore hussar dress, and officers of the Life Guard hussars, were entitled to wear 'gala' breeches at balls and other dismounted special occasions. These breeches had elaborate lace decoration on the fronts of the thighs in silver or gold, and did not necessarily agree with the colour of either the *Pelz* or Attila. Thus it was that the gala breeches of the 6th and 7th were poppy red and the 10th deep pink.

The dress headgear of the hussars was the busby or *Pelzmütze*; which was also worn in the field, usually with a reed green cover. For other ranks the busby was a short, almost cylindrical, black sealskin hat with a field sign in the state colours to the front upper edge. The officers' busby was taller and more voluminous and, until 1912 was of dark brown otter fur, a material which was then officially changed to grey opposum, but both types continued to be worn. Officers of the 17th wore a busby of black bearskin. Most busbies were fitted with a scroll in brass or white metal on which appeared the legend *Mit Gott für König und Vaterland*, meaning 'With God for King and Fatherland', but the 7th had only a 'WR I' royal cypher and the Life Guard hussars and the Saxon regiments had stars. The 1st and 2nd *Leib* and the 17th

Above.

Prussian Hussars, 1890s. Left to right: NCO *Leib-Husaren* Regiment Nr 2; Hussar Regiment Nr 3, parade dress; Regiment Nr 4 trumpeter; Regiment Nr 7; Major, Regiment Nr 11; Lieutenant, Regiment Nr 12; Regiment Nr 9; Second Lieutenant Regiment Nr 15. From *Nachträge und Berichtigungen Zum Deutschen Reichsheer.*

Right.

The *Dunkelblau* uniform of the 27th Nassau field artillery, as depicted c. 1900.

17th Brunswick were distinguished by a skull and crossbones badge. Beneath the right hand boss of the busby chin scales appeared a German national cockade in black, white and red. A further regimental distinction was the colourful cloth bag, worn on the left of the busby. For the Life Guard, 1st *Leib*, 3rd, 6th, 7th, 11th, 13th, 14th, 17th, and 18th the bag was red: white bags were worn by the 2nd *Leib* and 12th. Yellow was the bag colour for the 4th, 15th and 6th, whilst the 8th and 9th had bags of cornflower blue. For the 5th the colour was dark red; for the 10th deep pink; for the 19th crimson; and for the 20th light blue.

The hussars' alternative headgear, the undress cap

or *Mütze*, was almost equally magnificent. For officers and senior non-commissioned officers the hat had a leather peak, none for the other ranks. The cap piping was in the colour of the regimental lace, and the crown of the cap was of the same colour as the Attila, but the cap band was of a contrasting colour. These colours were: dark blue for the Life Guard and 3rd; red for the 1st *Leib*, 6th, 7th, 11th, 13th, 14th and 17th; black for the 2nd *Leib* and 5th; brown for 4th; cornflower blue for the 8th, 9th and 12th; pink for the 18th, 19th and 20th.

The lancer regiments or *Ulanen* may not have been quite so colourful as the hussars since all the Prussian and Württemberg Ulans wore blue in full dress, the Bavarians green, and the Saxons light blue, yet there were several traditional features in their dress which singled them out. Perhaps the most obvious was the continued use of a rather exaggerated form of the *Tschapka*, or square topped lance cap of Polish origin. This was of black laquered leather with a state badge on the skull section and, in full dress, a coloured cover on the upper part. The Ulan jacket or *Ulanka* was also of a distinctive pattern, being double-breasted, and having epaulettes with rounded ends rather than a plain shoulder strap and pointed cuffs.

Perhaps surprisingly the tubular steel lance was not unique to the *Ulanen*, having been universally issued to the cavalry prior to 1914. On the march it was carried with its butt resting in a socket on the stirrup and held on the crook of the arm by means of a sling. It was decorated with a pennant in the provincial colours: black and white for Prussia; blue and white for Bavaria; green and white for Saxony and in the case of non-commissioned officers, it was adorned with an eagle or state arms. The main regimental differences to the full dress uniforms of the *Ulanen* were as follows:

Ulan Regiment	Collar, cuffs and lapels	Epaulettes and cap cover	Buttons
1st Guard	Red (white lapels)	White	White metal
2nd Guard	Red	Red	Yellow metal
3rd Guard	Yellow	Yellow	White metal
1st	Red	White	Yellow metal
2nd	Red	Red	Yellow metal
3rd	Red	Yellow	Yellow metal
4th	Red	Light Blue	Yellow metal
5th	Red	White	White metal
6th	Red	Red	White metal
7th	Red	Yellow	White metal
8th	Red	Light Blue	White metal

9th	White	White	Yellow metal
10th	Crimson	Crimson	Yellow metal
11th	Yellow	Yellow	Yellow metal
12th	Light Blue	Light Blue	Yellow metal
13th	White	White	White metal
14th	Crimson	Crimson	White metal
15th	White	Yellow	White metal
16th	Light Blue	Light Blue	White metal
17th (Saxon)	Light blue uniform, crimson facings		
18th (Saxon)	Light blue uniform, crimson facings		

Left.

A squadron of *Jäger zu Pferde*. Uniform details include a standing collar to the jacket, long riding boots and a distinctive helmet. Notice the officer at the front of the unit and that the lance pennants of NCOs are adorned with an eagle. TRH Pictures.

Below.

Pre-war recruits at the Lockstedter Lager camp near Neumünster. The majority of the uniform is *Dunkelblau*, but grey *Pickelhaube* covers are worn; note the NCO with sword, peaked cap and lace on his coat collar. One man wears the grey greatcoat with the scarlet infantry collar patches. The rifles are obsolete G88 Mausers. SB.

Dress Uniforms 1900-1915 17

Bavarian Cavalry, 1890s. Left to right: *Schwere-Reiter* Regiment Nr 1, officer and Regiment Nr 2, Trooper in parade dress; *Ulanen* Regiment Nr 1 in greatcoat and *Ulanen* Regiment Nr 2, NCO; *Chevauleger* Regiment Nr 3, Lieutenant; *Chevauleger* Regiment Nr 1, Trooper in stable dress; *Chevauleger* Regiment Nr 4, Trooper in drill order; Riding School NCO. From *Nachträge und Berichtigungen zum Deutschen Reichsheer.*

19th (Württemberg) Blue uniform, red facings
20th (Württemberg) Blue uniform, yellow facings
21st (Saxon)   Light blue uniform, crimson facings
1st (Bavarian)   Green uniform, crimson facings
2nd (Bavarian)   Green uniform, crimson facings

The dragoon dress uniform was comparatively simple being a *Pickelhaube* worn with a cornflower blue *Waffenrock* and dark blue overalls. The jacket had a standing collar which, together with the Swedish cuffs, was distinctly coloured. These regimental colours were: red for the Guards and regiments 1, 5, 13, 17 and 20; black for 2, 6, 14, 18, 19 and 22; yellow for 4, 8, 16, 21 and 26; crimson for 11 and 12; pink for 3, 7 and 15 and white for 10 and 25. Hessian dragoons, like the Bavarian *Chevauleger,* were clad in green.

The *Jäger zu Pferde,* literally 'mounted rifles', were the newest horsed units in the Imperial German army, the first three bodies of which were raised to the status of regiments as recently as 1905. By 1914, however, a further 10 had been embodied bringing the total number to 13. A distinction was retained between those units raised before 1913 and those numbered eight to 13 which were raised on 1st October 1913. The 'old' units numbered one to seven wore a Cuirassier style *Waffenrock* whilst the jacket of the 'new' units was in the style of the dragoons. Although all the jackets were grey-green each regiment had its own facing colour:

Regiment	Facing Colour
1st *Königs*	White
2nd	Poppy Red
3rd	Lemon Yellow
4th	Light Blue
5th	Black
6th	Dark Blue
7th	Rose
8th	White
9th	Red
10th	Yellow

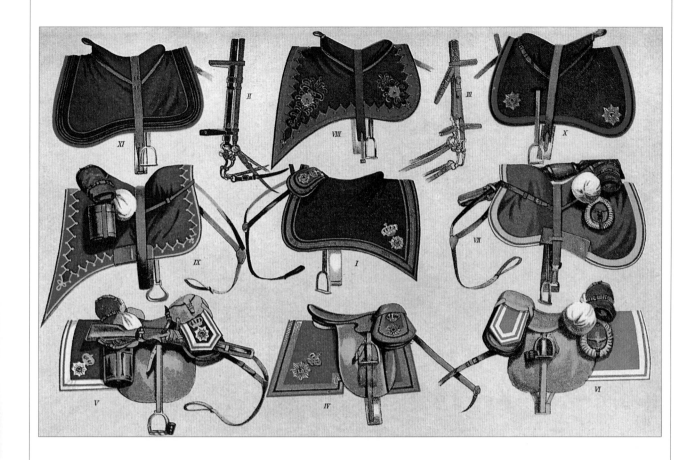

Above.

Prussian Horse Furniture, 1890s.

I)   General's parade shabraque.

II)   General's parade bridle.

III)   Cavalry officer's bridle for all except Hussar officers.

IV)   Parade shabraque *Garde du Corps* officers.

V)   Service saddle and equipment *Garde du Corps* and *Garde Kürassier*.

VI)   Line *Kürassier* service saddle and equipment.

VII)   Service saddle and equipment for dragoons.

VIII) Parade shabraque *Leib-Husaren* officers.

IX)   Service saddle and equipment, Hussars.

X)   Parade shabraque, officers of *Ulanen* Regiments.

XI)   Parade shabraque, line *Feld Artillerie* officers.

From Nachträge und Berichtigungen Zum Deutschen Reichsheer.

11th	Light Blue
12th	Black
13th	Dark Blue

Other ranks wore the unit's regimental number on the dress uniform shoulder strap, but as Kaiser Wilhelm was the colonel in chief of the 1st these wore the cypher 'WR II' in yellow or gilt instead. A *Litewka* style working jacket in light grey was worn by officers and also by other ranks of the first seven regiments.

The officers' *Litewka* was double-breasted, the other ranks' single-breasted and fly fronted. Both had light green collar patches. Officers could also wear a grey-green frock coat or *Überrock*. Plain grey-green *Reithosen* or breeches were the usual mounted rifle legwear after 1911, though white gala trousers and black 'walking out' trousers for officers were not unknown.

A differentiation between the old and new *Jäger zu Pferde* regiments was also maintained in the headgear. The first seven regiments all wore the *Helm*, or helmet, of blackened polished steel in cuirassier style. Fittings for this headgear were in silver for officers and white metal for other ranks. Officers were also allowed to purchase and wear an 'extra helm' of brightly polished steel. Though officers of regiments eight to 13 also wore the *Helm*, the other ranks of these formations wore a black leather *Pickelhaube* with fittings of yellow metal.

Field Service Uniform

Field Service *Waffenrock*, and the field grey uniform of 1910

Experiments with *feldgrau* or 'field grey' uniforms with a view to producing a costume good from the point of view of concealment, yet smart and practical under the conditions of modern war, had begun in the German army as early as 1907. This departure was late by the standards of the British who had adopted a universal khaki service dress in 1902, or the Russians who took up a greenish khaki in 1907, yet it was well ahead of the Belgians and of the French who in 1914 had not yet abandoned their blue uniforms and famous red trousers. Moreover the use of grey and green uniforms in Germany and Prussia was not without precedent. Prussian reservists had worn grey in the Napoleonic wars, and certain units in undress, and others in full dress, most notably *Jäger* and *Jäger zu Pferde*, had been wearing greens and greys well before 1907.

It appears that by 1908 as a part of the first widespread practical tests some units were issued with field grey uniforms of a smooth heavy woollen cloth with an off-white cotton lining. The lace and buttons with which these first field grey uniforms were decorated seem to have been identical with those in use on the contemporary *Dunkelblau* uniforms. The experiment must have been accounted a success for in the spring of 1910 the Kaiser signed orders for the general introduction of field grey, and soon after the active regiments were sporting a light field grey. It was not possible to re-equip all the reserve, *Landwehr* and *Landsturm* formations overnight, and photographic evidence suggests that many of these bodies continued to use dark blue uniforms out of the front line as late as 1916. Officially, coloured dress uniforms were abandoned in 1915 at the same time as the introduction of a new field grey full dress for use after the war. Interestingly there is some evidence to suggest that a small minority of units actually campaigned in blue in 1914 before they could be reclothed.

The popular picture of a monolithic German army, universally clad in identical Model 1910 uniform at the outbreak of war is undoubtedly wrong, partly because of the many state variations and because many types of troops carried over distinctions from the full dress of their particular arm of service. In this respect the German uniform of 1914 was more truly a 'service' version of the existing uniform than the British Service Dress, which bore little relationship to its full dress equivalent.

Thus it was that the most common of the 1910-type jackets was a field service version of the *Waffenrock*, also referred to as a *Feldrock*. This was field grey for the majority of the infantry and cavalry and grey-green, *graugrün*, for the *Jäger*, mounted and dismounted, and for the machine-gun detachments. The basic garment was a fairly loose fitting coat closed by eight nickel or tombak (zinc-copper alloy) buttons in front and in the skirts were pockets which were fastened with buttoned flaps. The collar was of a stand and fall variety. Issue jackets were usually stamped internally with the letters 'B.A.' signifying *Bekleidungsamt* or 'clothing department', followed by Roman numerals denoting the Army Corps and a date. Unit marks are also encountered where a number followed by 'J.R.' or 'I.R.' shows a specific infantry regiment, and the prefix 'B' before such a number signifies Bavarian. Scarlet piping to the *Waffenrock* denoted the infantry and machine-gunners, green piping the *Jäger*, and green piping to the body of the jacket with black collar and cuff piping the *Schützen* and 2nd Guard machine-gun detachment. Artillery and pioneers had red piping to the body of the jacket with black collar and cuff piping; medical troops had dark blue piping.

Officers' uniforms were not usually issue garments, being paid for by the officer concerned and made to

Prussian *Vizefeldwebel* Maxiner, pictured at Bad Ems, February 1915. Maxiner wears the *Dienstmütze*; light grey greatcoat over field grey uniform and belt, boots and gloves. Note that the *Vizefeldwebel* is a portepée rank, so that a sword and knot are carried in addition to the distinctive bars of lace on the jacket and greatcoat collars. SB.

A philosophical view of the conscript's journey into uniform: 'he who has choice has pain'.

order. As might be expected the result was a uniform of better quality and fit. Rank insignia were carried on the shoulder, along with any regimental device. Staff officers wore red collar patches. General officers were distinguished by a special pattern of service dress jacket, this had red piped turn back or 'roll' cuffs, and integral breast pockets with flaps. This jacket also had distinctive long, red collar patches on which appeared a special embroidery which differed according to state. Other minor variations are apparent in photographs. On formal occasions the General officers' jacket was worn with distinctive field grey trousers which had triple red stripes down the legs. The outbreak of war saw the recall of many senior officers who had not been active in the past four years, and so it was that a number of older Generals began the war in obsolete uniform. Hindenburg himself set off for the Eastern Front wearing the *Litewka* of the 3rd Guards regiment.

The jackets worn by the *Kürassiere*, *Dragoner*, and *Jäger zu Pferde* were similar to the *Waffenrock* of the infantry but had a stand up collar and used regimentally coloured pipings. The collars and cuffs of these garments (except those of the Dragons) were also trimmed with *Bortenbesatz* or regimentally patterned braid. Hussar units wore a field grey *Attila* rather than the *Waffenrock*, complete with five looped bars of dull grey braid on the chest, and shoulder cords rather than straps, whilst *Ulanen*, or lancers, wore a field grey *Ulanka*. This garment was a double-breasted tunic with two rows of seven buttons, pointed cuffs, and a stand up collar. Chaplains were exceptional in that they tended to wear a long frock coat.

Thus far the picture was reasonably straightforward, but it was further complicated by differences to buttons, cuffs, skirt ornaments, *Litzen*, and shoulder straps. Jacket buttons were of two main types; embossed with a lion for Bavarian units and otherwise usually bearing the state crown of the units' origin. A small version of the button was used to fasten the shoulder straps. The majority of regiments started the war with tombak buttons; tombak being an alloy of

An unauthorised private photograph showing General Hermann von François, commander of 1 Corps during an Eastern Front briefing. François gained a reputation as a difficult and aggressive commander, but was arguably one of the driving forces behind the victory at Tannenberg which made Hindenburg's reputation. SB.

zinc and copper which had a reddish brass appearance. Certain units, mainly of the Guard, wore nickel buttons. Fairly quickly, however, such distinction was eroded by the fact that many new jackets were produced with dull grey, painted buttons and that other alloys or war-time substitute materials, generically known as *Kriegsmettall*, came into use.

The main four cuff patterns of the *Waffenrock* were the Brandenburg, Swedish, Saxon (sometimes referred to as German), and French. The Brandenburg was the commonest, having an oblong vertical flap with three buttons. The Saxon which had two buttons arranged one below and one above the piping was used by Saxon units excepting the Saxon Grenadier regiments 100 and 101. The Swedish cuff had two buttons arranged horizontally below the piping and was worn amongst others by senior officers, machine-gun units, many of the Guards, Baden *Leib Grenadier* regiment 109, Württemberg Grenadier regiments 119 and 123,

the aforementioned Saxon Grenadier units and the field artillery, *Kürassiere* and dragoons. The French cuff which had three vertical buttons mounted with *Litzen* was worn by the *Garde Schützen*, and the by the 2nd Guard machine gun detachment. The usual rear skirt ornamentation on the original 1910-type *Waffenrock* had four buttons, two down either side, whilst the Saxon arrangement had only two buttons and a different pattern of piping.

Collar and cuff *Litzen*, or small decorative bars of material of a contrasting colour, were traditionally associated with the Guards and other senior regiments of the army. Collar *Litzen* were worn on the collar and extended as far as a point level with the shoulder strap button; cuff *Litzen* were placed one on each button, three horizontally on a Brandenburg cuff, two vertically on a Swedish cuff. The three main patterns were 'double', 'single' and 'Old Prussian' which came to a point at one end. Usually *Litzen* were white with a red centre line, the main exceptions being Fusilier regiment 80, which had no centre line; the Guard and 14th *Jäger* battalions which had green; and the *Garde Schützen* and 2nd machine-gun detachment which had black. Guard machine-gunners were also unusual in that the area between their double yellow *Litzen* was infilled red or black, depending on whether they were

Saxon infantrymen on the Western Front. The features which distinguish their uniform from that of other states are: the form of the cuff on the *Waffenrock*; the Saxon white, green, white, lower cap cockade which here is covered by a grey camouflage band; the Saxon belt buckle; and the form of the rear skirts of the jacket. TRH Pictures.

of the 1st or 2nd detachment. The 5th Guard Grenadiers, the *Garde Jäger* and *Schützen*, had yellow *Litzen*.

Old Prussian *Litzen* were worn by the 5th Guards, both the *zu Fuß* and Grenadier regiments, as well as the Fusilier regiment Nr. 90. Single *Litzen* were worn by line Grenadier regiments. Guard regiments 1–4 inclusive, both of the *zu Fuß*, and Grenadiers wore double *Litzen*, as did the Guard Fusiliers, Grenadier regiments 89,100,101,109, 115, 119 and 123 and the Guard *Jäger*, *Schützen* and machine-gun detachments.

Both unit designations and Army Corps could be revealed by the button down shoulder strap of the original 1910 *Waffenrock* and during the war the taking of German shoulder straps from prisoners or captured clothing provided enemy intelligence with a vital source of information. The shoulder strap piping of Guard regiments was an indicator of seniority; 1st

regiments having white; 2nd regiments red; 3rd regiments yellow; 4th regiments light blue and the Guard Fusiliers wore lemon yellow shoulder strap piping. *Jäger* battalions wore green shoulder strap piping on the *Waffenrock* and Guard *Schützen* red. Air Service, Telegraph and Communications troops had light grey piping. In the infantry this peripheral stripe of colour indicated the Army Corps:

Army Corps	Shoulder strap piping
I, II, IX, X, XII (1st Saxon), I Bavarian	White
III, IV, XI, XIII, XV, XIX (2nd Saxon), II Bavarian	Red
V, VI, XVI, XVII, III Bavarian	Yellow
VII, VIII, XVIII, XX	Light Blue
XXI	Light Green

A full listing of regiments in 1914 and their shoulder strap pipings, including exceptions to the general rules, is given near the end of this chapter.

In the centre of the shoulder strap appeared the regimental number, or particularly in the case of senior regiments, a cypher or monogram, all of which were stitched in red. So it was that the *Waffenrock*

General Erich von Falkenhayn (left), pictured during his time as commander of Ninth Army in the war in Romania. Falkenhayn served as Minister of War in 1914, taking an active role as Chief of General Staff after von Moltke's offensive in the West had ground to a halt. Falkenhayn gambled both his career and the German Army on the February 1916 offensive at Verdun, which he termed a 'Meuse mill' designed to 'bleed' the French 'to death'. Half a million casualties and ten million shells later, it was clear, as Rupprecht of Bavaria observed, that Falkenhayn had lost 'the big picture' in the *Ermattungsstrategie* or campaign of attrition. Falkenhayn was replaced by Hindenburg in August 1916 and redeployed to less crucial tasks. Note Falkenhayn's single-breasted greatcoat and the undress *Litewka* worn by the officer with him. IWMQ 23726

Colonel-General Alexander von Kluck wearing the uniform of a Guards officer. Kluck commanded First Army on the right wing of the drive to the West in 1914, meeting the British at Mons. Kluck was wounded in 1915 and later retired. IWM Q 45327.

shoulder strap of the *Württembergisches Grenadier Regiment Königin Olga*, though the unit numbered 119 in the regimental series, actually bore a crown over the monogram 'O'. *Garde Grenadier Regiment Nr 1*, as the *Kaiser Alexander* regiment, bore an 'A' under an imperial crown and a small number '1'. Fusilier regiment 34 was technically the Pommeranian *Füsilier Regiment Konigin Viktoria von Schweden*, and thus bore a stylised, crowned 'V'. British intelligence sources identified well over 50 such cyphers or monograms

used in the field, and depicted them in the staff handbook issued on the German army. This, though useful to the Allied cause, was not an especially astonishing feat since approximately 90 such symbols were published by Paul Meybauer in his *Helmwappen und Namenszüge der Deutschen Armee*.

Distinct from these monograms but also placed on the shoulder straps were a series of letters and symbols, again usually in red, which denoted troop types. Grenades were worn by the artillery, a hunting horn by the Saxon *Jäger* and *Schützen*, and a crossed pick and shovel by the Saxon pioneers; aircraft units had stylised wings and propellor. An italic 'L' for *Luftschiff* was worn by balloon and airship units; 'E' for *Eisenbahn* by railway troops; 'T' by telegraph units; a 'K' by mechanical transport units; and a 'V' by experimental companies. One other distinction applied to shoulder straps served to denote the *Einjährige* or One Year volunteers, the generally affluent young men who agreed to serve for one year and to pay their own expenses and then join the officer

An *Eiserner Kreuz* winner of Bavarian Infanterie-Regiment Nr 13 'Franz Joseph I', pictured at Nürnberg. The man's *Waffenrock* has collar piping and red numerals on the shoulder straps; the buttons bear the Bavarian lion. The iron cross was in two main classes, first and second, though a 'Grand Cross' was awarded four times and worn by the Kaiser himself. The medal was a cross patée bearing a crown, the letter 'W' and, for the Great War, the date 1914; the ribbon was black and white. The second class award, shown here, was given freely during the conflict sometimes to whole units at a time, with the result that the total awarded by the end of the war was over 5,000,000. P. Hannon.

A *Gefreiter* of *Grenadier-Regiment König Friedrich der Große* (3. *Ostpreußisches*) Nr 4, pictured at Rastenburg in East Prussia c. 1914. The collar of the field grey *Waffenrock* has single *Litzen* and a small rank button; horizontal *Litzen* are also worn on the buttons of the Brandenburg cuffs. The white belt is for parade or ceremonial use. P. Hannon.

reserve, rather than do the usual term of compulsory service. In the case of these men the shoulder strap piping consisted of a twisted cord of state colours: black and white for Prussia; blue, yellow and red for Mecklenburg; white and light blue for Bavaria; white and green for Saxony; red and white for Hesse; white, black and red for Württemberg.

The *Landsturm* had their own set of shoulder straps according to arm of service: blue for infantry; black for pioneers; scarlet for field artillery; and yellow for foot artillery. These, unlike those of the regulars, bore no numbers; instead, *Landsturm* units were differentiated by dull brass numerals worn on the collar. The Army

Corps number appeared as Roman numerals, the battalion in Arabic numerals. Thus, for example, the collar numerals 'XI 22' would indicate the 22nd *Landsturm* battalion of the 11th Thuringia and Hesse-Nassau Army Corps District; 'XIV 33' was the abbreviation for the 33rd *Landsturm* battalion of the 14th Baden Army Corps district.

It can be little wonder that the 1910 system of distinctions as applied to the *Waffenrock*, complex and time consuming to produce, potentially confusing to friends, and a mine of information to a diligent enemy, soon began to break down. Expansion of the army and exigencies of war soon meant that there were not enough field grey *Waffenröck* of the right types to go round, and that men transferred from second echelon units to the front, or called up from reserve, brought with them out of date or incorrect garments. Very rapidly, corners were cut and jackets began to appear with less than their full complement of fussy

distinctions. These jackets, which were apparently quite common at the time, have since become known by a number of descriptions including 'interim', 'Simplified model 1910' or even 'model 1914'. Amongst the features most frequently deleted were the ornamental cuffs, commonly replaced by a plain deep turn back and the false skirt flaps at the back. Shoulder strap pipings were also frequently omitted, the result being a plain field grey strap with just the number or cypher of the regiment in red.

The service trousers or *Tuchhose* of the infantry were, in theory, matched to the colour of the jacket; they were to be piped red, or green for *Jäger* units. For the bulk of the cavalry, field grey *Reithose* or breeches with red piping were prescribed; the *Reithose* of the *Jäger zu Pferde* had green piping, and those of the hussars a braid stripe at the seam. In practice, however, the trousers actually worn by many of the troops were soon of other kinds. New trousers were officially introduced in *Steingrau*, or stone grey, but there were a number of other innovations. It is well known that corduroy trousers were popular with mountain troops, but is less often appreciated that corduroy was also a standby used by many reservist and *Landwehr* units in grey, brown and possibly other colours. Officers, who had often indulged in the most

exaggerated of breeches, were instructed in 1915 to keep the width and cut similar to those of the rank and file. Presumably the intention was not only to stem their sartorial extravagances but to prevent the enemy snipers' job from becoming too easy.

As has been noted above, in connection with dress uniform, greatcoats of 1901 or 1907 Pattern were worn in inclement weather, and on active service over the field grey uniform. The 1901 coat was described in a contemporary French work as an:

'overcoat of grey cloth closed over the breast by a single row of six metal buttons and adjusted to the waist behind by a cloth strap. It has a falling collar under which is attached a small hood of cotton cloth. The sleeves terminate in wide facings which can be turned down to cover the hands'. The coat had two pockets in the skirts, and the upper part of the coat was lined with linen.

The new greatcoat, introduced in 1907, was light grey and lacked the concealed hood. It was, however, adorned with the *Mantelpatten*: oblong coloured patches either side of the collar, with small *Litzen* where appropriate. The colour of these patches varied according to unit: the infantry and Prussian *Jäger* patches were red; the patches of the

Infantryman Paul Anders of *Badisches Infanterie-Regiment Nr 170*, pictured in a street standing by the discarded packs of his comrades prior to departure for the front, in 1914. He wears textbook uniform with red numerals on the *Pickelhaube* cover, 1909 type ammunition pouches and a torch attached to his buttons. Within a matter of weeks Anders would be posted as missing. P. Hannon.

Prussian troops pictured relaxing at Esslingen c. 1914. The *Jäger*, on the left of the group, wears the shako with Prussian eagle and a fatigue jacket. SB.

Bavarian and Mecklenburg *Jäger* were green; those of the *Schützen* were black. The field artillery had black patches with red piping. For the cavalry the greatcoat collar patch generally agreed with the regimental distinctive colour, but there were a number of exceptions. Chief amongst these were the patches of the *Jäger zu Pferde* which were universally green; and those of the hussars which mainly agreed with the colour of the busby bag, except for the 2nd and 12th which had patches in the colour of their dress jackets and the 20th Hussars which had field grey patches with light blue edge piping. NCO collar patches were further distinguished by a band, or bands, of lace.

New and properly fitted, the *Feldgrau* uniform could appear extremely smart. When this was not the case, or worn by a less than perfect specimen of humanity, it could be just as ridiculous, if not more so,

than the military dress of other nations. Such was the observation of Gustav Ebelshauser, a Swiss serving with 1st Battalion Bavarian Infantry Regiment Nr 17, *Orff*: according to his memoirs one man was so portly that the company tailor had to move his buttons right to the edge of his jacket, and the seat of his trousers had to be enlarged to 'monumental width' by the addition of a panel of material of a noticeably different colour. In another instance a man wore trousers so large that it was speculated that his whole body would fit inside them, whilst his jacket was voluminous enough to 'hold three'. It was bitterly remarked that the carelessness of the quartermasters made this particular company look more like 'clowns in a circus than soldiers about to fight'.

Field Marshal von Mackensen (left), commander of the army of occupation in Romania wearing the field uniform of the *1 Leib-Husaren-Regiment* during an award ceremony at Bucharest in 1917. His adjutant is in the act of decorating a soldier of *3 Kurhessisches Infanterie-Regiment von Wittich Nr 83*; whilst in the background a hussar receives a medal from a Guards officer. IWM 24006.

THE REGULAR ARMY AND ITS DISTINCTIONS IN FIELD DRESS 1914

INFANTRY

Prussian Guard	Shoulder strap piping	Buttons	Litzen	Corps
1. Garde-Regiment zu Fuß	White	Nickel	White	Garde
2. Garde-Regiment zu Fuß	Red	Tombak	White	Garde
3. Garde-Regiment zu Fuß	Yellow	Tombak	White	Garde
4. Garde-Regiment zu Fuß	L. Blue	Tombak	White	Garde
5. Garde-Regiment zu Fuß	White	Nickel	White	Garde
Garde-Füsilier Regiment	Yellow	Nickel	White	Garde

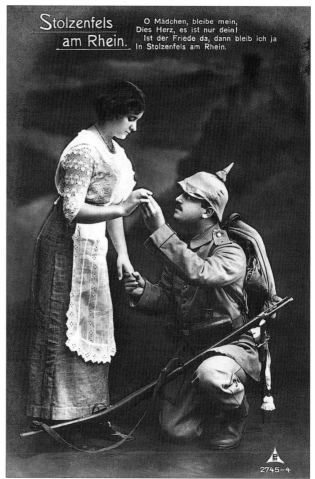

A study of a young *Unteroffizier* of *Badisches Leib-Grenadier-Regiment Nr 109* in walking out dress, c. 1914. The collar of the jacket has both rank lace and *Litzen*; the cuffs are of the Swedish type decorated with vertical Litzen. The shoulder strap bears the regimental crown motif in red and is piped white. Notice also the formal peaked cap and the long S 98 bayonet worn with an NCO's knot. P. Hannon.

A 1915 postcard picture of an infantryman and his sweetheart which contrives to be patriotic, romantic and an advertisement for civic pride. The verse reads, 'Oh girl, stay mine, this heart is always yours! When the peace comes, then will I stay here, in Stolzenfels am Rhein'. The rifle is an ancient studio prop dating back to the 1860s. SB.

Kaiser Alexander Garde-Grenadier Regiment Nr 1	White	Tombak	White	Garde
Kaiser Franz Garde-Grenadier Regiment Nr 2	Red	Tombak	White	Garde
Königin Elizabeth Garde-Grenadier Regiment Nr 3	Yellow	Tombak	White	Garde
Königin Augusta Garde-Grenadier Regiment Nr 4	L. Blue	Tombak	White	Garde
Garde-Grenadier Regiment Nr 5	White	Tombak	Yellow	Garde

Other differences: the collar decorations of *Garde zu Fuß* regiments 1-4, *Garde Grenadier* regiments 1-4, and the *Garde Füsilier* regiment were double *Litzen* with a red centre line. *Garde zu Fuß* Nr 5, and *Garde Grenadier* Nr 5 wore the Old Prussian *Litzen* with a red centre line. The *Garde zu Fuß* and the *Garde Füsilier* wore no shoulder strap device whilst the *Garde Grenadiers* all had their own monograms with crowns in red. Regimental staff and I Battalion of *Garde zu Fuß* Nr 1 wore the motto *Semper Talis* on the helmet plates. Swedish cuffs were worn by the *Garde zu Fuß* regiments 1–4, and the *Garde Füsiliers*, Brandenburg cuffs were worn by the remainder.

Prussian Grenadier Regiments	Shoulder strap piping	Buttons	Litzen	Corps
Grenadier-Regiment Kronprinz (1. Ostpreußisches) Nr 1	White	Tombak	White	I
Grenadier-Regiment König Friedrich Wilhelm IV. (1. Pommersches) Nr 2	White	Tombak	White	II
Grenadier-Regiment König Friedrich Wilhelm I. (2. Ostpreußisches) Nr 3	White	Tombak	White	I
Grenadier-Regiment König Friedrich der Goße (3. Ostpreußisches) Nr 4	White	Tombak	White	I
Grenadier-Regiment König Friedrich I. (4. Ostpreußisches) Nr 5	Yellow	Tombak	White	XVII
Grenadier-Regiment Graf Kleist von Nollendorf (1. Westpreußisches) Nr 6	Yellow	Tombak	White	V
Grenadier-Regiment König Wilhelm I. (2. Westpreußiches) Nr 7	Yellow	Tombak	Yellow	V

The warrior's departure. A sentimental postcard depicting a member of the *Landsturm* **taking leave of his family; note the traditional flowers and the distinctive cylindrical cap with cross.** SB.

A mounted *Unteroffizier* of a Train unit. Note the greatcoat with collar lace and divided skirt. Mounted troops were also issued with canvas capes. TRH Pictures. (T. Neville)

Leib Grenadier-Regiment König Friedrich Wilhelm III (1. Brandenburgisches) Nr 8	Red	Tombak	White	III
Colberg Grenadier-Regiment Graf Gneisenau (2. Pommersches) Nr 9	White	Tombak	-	II
Grenadier-Regiment König FriedrichWilhelm II (1. Schlesisches) Nr 10	Yellow	Tombak	-	VI
Grenadier-Regiment König Friedrich III (2. Schlesisches) Nr 11	Yellow	Tombak	White	VI
Grenadier-Regiment Prinz Karl von Preußen (2. Brandenburgisches) Nr 12	Red	Tombak	-	III

Other differences: monograms with crowns in red were worn on the shoulder straps of the Prussian grenadier regiments with the exception of Nr 6, Nr 9 and Nr 12, which wore their respective numerals. The Grenadier regiments wore only single *Litzen*, their cuffs were of the 'Brandenburg' type. The date '1655' appeared on the helmets and officers' sword grips of the Grenadier Regiment Nr 1, similarly the date '1626' was used by Grenadier Regiment Nr 2. Regiment Nr 7 carried the date '22 März 1797' on their helmets in commemoration of the birthday of their patron, whilst Nr 9 had the inscription 'Colberg 1807'.

Other regiments of Prussia and the smaller states	Shoulder strap piping	Buttons	Litzen	Corps
Infanterie-Regiment Herwarth von Bittenfeld (1. Westfälisches) Nr 13	L. Blue	Tombak	-	VII
Infanterie-Regiment Graf Schwerin (3. Pommersches) Nr 14	White	Tombak	-	II
Infanterie-Regiment Prinz Friedrich der Niederlande (2. Westfälisches) Nr 15	L. Blue	Tombak	-	VII
Infanterie-Regiment Freiherr von Sparr (3. Westfälisches) Nr 16	L. Blue	Tombak	-	VII
Infanterie-Regiment Graf Barfuß (4. Westfälisches) Nr 17	L. Green	Tombak	-	XXI
Infanterie-Regiment von Grolman (1. Posensches) Nr 18	L. Blue	Tombak	-	XX
Infanterie-Regiment von Coubière (2. Posensches) Nr 19	Yellow	Tombak	-	V
Infanterie-Regiment Graf Tauentzien von Wittenberg (3. Brandenburgisches) Nr 20	Red	Tombak	-	III
Infanterie-Regiment von Borcke (4. Pommersches) Nr 21	Yellow	Tombak	-	XVII
Infanterie-Regiment Keith (1. Oberschlesisches) Nr 22	Yellow	Tombak	-	VI
Infanterie-Regiment von Winterfeldt (2. Oberschlesisches) Nr 23	Yellow	Tombak	-	VI
Infanterie-Regiment Großherzog Friedrich Franz II von Mecklenburg-Schwerin (4. Brandenburgisches) Nr 24	Red	Tombak	-	III
Infanterie-Regiment von Lützow (1. Rheinisches) Nr 25	L. Blue	Tombak	-	VIII
Infanterie-Regiment Fürst Leopold von Anhalt-Dessau (1. Magdeburgisches) Nr 26	Red	Tombak	-	IV
Infanterie-Regiment Prinz Louis Ferdinand von Preußen (2. Magdeburgisches) Nr 27	Red	Tombak	-	IV
Infanterie-Regiment von Goeben (2. Rheinisches) Nr 28	L. Blue	Tombak	-	VIII

Infanterie-Regiment von Horn *(3. Rheinisches) Nr 29*	L. Blue	Tombak	-	VIII
Infanterie-Regiment Graf Werder *(4. Rheinisches) Nr 30*	Yellow	Tombak	-	XVI
Infanterie-Regiment Graf Bose *(1. Thüringisches) Nr 31*	White	Tombak	-	IX
2 Thüringisches Infanterie-Regiment *Nr 32*	Red	Tombak	-	XI
Füsilier-Regiment Graf Roon *(Ostpreußisches) Nr 33*	White	Tombak	-	I
Füsilier-Regiment Königin Viktoria von Schweden *(Pommersches) Nr 34*	White	Tombak	-	II
Füsilier-Regiment Prinz Heinrich von Preußen *(Brandenburgisches) Nr 35*	Red	Tombak	-	III
Füsilier-Regiment General-Feldmarschall Graf von *Blumenthal (Magdeburgisches) Nr 36*	Red	Tombak	-	IV
Füsilier-Regiment von Steinmetz *(Westpreußisches) Nr 37*	Yellow	Tombak	-	V
Füsiler-Regiment General-Feldmarschall Graf Moltke *(Schlesisches) Nr 38*	Yellow	Tombak	-	VI
Niederrheinisches Füsilier *Regiment Nr 39*	Blue	Tombak	-	VII
Füsilier-Regiment Fürst Karl Anton von *Hohenzollern (Hohenzollernsches) Nr 40*	L. Blue	Tombak	-	XIV
Infanterie-Regiment von Boyen *(5. Ostpreußisches) Nr 41*	White	Tombak	-	I
Infanterie-Regiment Prinz Moritz von Anhalt-Dessau *(5. Pommersches) Nr 42*	White	Tombak	-	II
Infanterie-Regiment Herzog Karl von *Mecklenburg-Strelitz (6. Ostpreußisches) Nr 43*	White	Tombak	-	I
Infanterie-Regiment Graf Dönhoff *(7. Ostpreußisches) Nr 44*	White	Tombak	-	I
8. Ostpreußisches Infanterie-Regiment Nr 45	White	Tombak	-	I
Infanterie-Regiment Graf Kirchbach *(1. Niederschleisisches) Nr 46*	Yellow	Tombak	-	V

A sentimental, though tolerably accurate, postcard of a Ulan and his sweetheart, spring 1915. The uniform includes a scarlet piped field grey *Ulanka* and the *Tschapka* with cover.

An officer of *Garde Ulanen* Regiment Nr 3, as depicted in an advertisement for *Feldgrau* Champagne!

Infanterie-Regiment König Ludwig III von Bayern (2. Niederschleisches) Nr 47	Yellow	Tombak	-	V
Infanterie-Regiment von Stülpnagel (5. Brandenburgisches) Nr 48	Red	Tombak	-	III
6. Pommersches Infanterie-Regiment Nr 49	White	Tombak	-	II
3. Niederschlesisches Infanterie-Regiment Nr 50	Yellow	Tombak	-	V
4. Niederschlesisches Infanterie-Regiment Nr 51	Yellow	Tombak	-	VI
Infanterie-Regiment von Alvensleben (6. Brandenburgisches) Nr 52	Red	Tombak	-	III
5. Westfälisches Infanterie-Regiment Nr 53	Blue	Tombak	-	VII
Infanterie-Regiment von der Goltz (7. Pommersches) Nr 54	White	Tombak	-	II
Infanterie-Regiment Graf Bülow von Dennewitz (6. Westfälisches) Nr 55	L. Blue	Tombak	-	VII

**Greatcoated artillerymen push a howitzer through the snow of
an Eastern Front birch wood, 1915.** SB.

Infanterie-Regiment Vogel von Falckenstein (7. Westfälisches) Nr 56	Blue	Tombak	-	VII
Infanterie-Regiment Herzog Ferdinand von Braunschweig (8. Westfälisches) Nr 57	L. Blue	Tombak	-	VII
3. Posensches Infanterie-Regiment Nr 58	Yellow	Tombak	-	V
Infanterie-Regiment Freiherr Hiller von Gärtringen (4. Posensches) Nr 59	L. Blue	Tombak	-	XX
Infanterie-Regiment Markgraf Karl (7. Brandenburgisches) Nr 60	L. Green	Tombak	-	XXI
Infanterie-Regiment von der Marwitz (8. Pommersches) Nr 61	Yellow	Tombak	-	XVII
3. Oberschlesisches Infanterie-Regiment Nr 62	Yellow	Tombak	-	VI
4. Oberschlesisches Infanterie-Regiment Nr 63	Yellow	Tombak	-	VI
Infanterie-Regiment General-Feldmarschall Prinz Friedrich Karl von Preußen (8. Brandenburgisches) Nr 64	Red	Tombak	-	III

5. Rheinisches Infanterie-Regiment Nr 65	L. Blue	Tombak	-	VIII
3. Magdeburgisches Infanterie-Regiment Nr 66	Red	Tombak	-	IV
4. Magdeburgisches Infanterie-Regiment Nr 67	Yellow	Tombak	-	XVI
6. Rheinisches Infanterie-Regiment Nr 68	L. Blue	Tombak	-	VIII
7. Rheinisches Infanterie-Regiment Nr 69	L. Blue	Tombak	-	VIII
8. Rheinisches Infanterie-Regiment Nr 70	L. Green	Tombak	-	XXI
3. Thüringisches Infanterie-Regiment Nr 71	Red	Tombak	-	XI
4. Thüringisches Infanterie-Regiment Nr 72	Red	Tombak	-	IV
Füsilier-Regiment General-Feldmarschall Prinz Albrecht von Preußen (Hannoversches) Nr 73	White	Tombak	-	X
1. Hannoversches Infanterie-Regiment Nr 74	White	Tombak	-	X
Infanterie-Regiment Bremen (1. Hanseatisches) Nr 75	White	Tombak	-	IX
Infanterie-Regiment Hamburg (2. Hanseatisches) Nr 76	White	Tombak	-	IX
2. Hannoversches Infanterie-Regiment Nr 77	White	Tombak	-	X
Infanterie-Regiment Herzog Friedrich Wilhelm von Braunschweig (Ostfriesisches) Nr 78	White	Tombak	-	X
Infanterie-Regiment von Voights-Rhetz (3. Hannoversches) Nr 79	White	Tombak	-	X
Füsilier-Regiment von Gersdorf (Kurhessisches) Nr 80	L. Blue	Nickel	White	XVIII
Infanterie-Regiment Landgraf Friedrich I von Hessen-Cassel (1. Kurhessisches) Nr 81	L. Blue	Tombak	-	XVIII
2. Kurhessisches Infanterie-Regiment Nr 82	Red	Tombak	-	XI
Infanterie-Regiment von Wittich (3. Kurhessisches) Nr 83	Red	Tombak	-	XI
Infanterie-Regiment von Manstein (Schlewigsches) Nr 84	White	Tombak	-	IX
Infanterie-Regiment Herzog von Holstein (Holsteinsches) Nr 85	White	Tombak	-	IX
Füsilier-Regiment Königin (Schleswig-Holsteinsches) Nr 86	White	Tombak	-	IX
1. Nassauisches Infanterie-Regiment Nr 87	L. Blue	Tombak	-	XVIII
2. Nassauisches Infanterie-Regiment Nr 88	L. Blue	Tombak	-	XVIII

Großherzoglich Mecklenburgisches Grenadier Regiment Nr. 89	White	Nickel	White	IX
Großherzoglich Mecklenburgisches Füsilier Regiment Nr 90 Kaiser Wilhelm	White	Nickel	-	IX
Oldenburgisches Infanterie-Regiment Nr 91	White	Tombak	-	X
Braunschweigisches Infanterie-Regiment Nr 92	White	Tombak	-	X
Anhaltisches Infanterie-Regiment Nr 93	Red	Tombak	-	IV
Infanterie-Regiment Großherzog von Sachsen (5. Thüringisches) Nr 94	Red	Tombak	-	XI
6. Thüringisches Infanterie-Regiment Nr 96	Red	Tombak	-	XI
1. Oberrheinisches Infanterie-Regiment Nr 97	L. Green	Tombak	-	XXI
Metzer Infanterie-Regiment Nr 98	Yellow	Tombak	-	XVI
2. Oberrheinisches Infanterie-Regiment Nr 99	Red	Tombak	-	XV
1. Badisches Leib-Grenadier-Regiment Nr 109	White	Nickel	White	XIV
2. Badisches Grenadier-Regiment Kaiser Wilhelm 1. Nr 110	White	Tombak	-	XIV
Infanterie-Regiment Markgraf Ludwig Wilhelm (3. Badisches) Nr 111	Red	Tombak	-	XIV
4. Badisches Infanterie-Regiment Prinz Wilhelm Nr 112	L. Green	Tombak	-	XIV
5. Badisches Infanterie-Regiment Nr 113.	Blue	Tombak	-	XIV
6. Badisches Infanterie-Regiment Kaiser Friedrich III. Nr 114	L. Green	Tombak	-	XIV
Leibgarde-Infanterie-Regiment (1. Großherzoglich Hessisches) Nr 115	Red	Tombak	White	XVIII
Infanterie-Regiment Kaiser Wilhelm (2. Großherzoglich Hessisches) Nr 116	White	Tombak	-	XVIII
Infanterie-Leibregiment Großherzogin (3. Großherzoglich Hessisches) Nr 117	Blue	Tombak	-	XVIII
Infanterie-Regiment Prinz Karl (4. Großherzoglich Hessisches) Nr 118	Yellow	Tombak	-	XVIII
Danziger Infanterie-Regiment Nr 128	Yellow	Tombak	-	XVII
3. Westpreußisches Infanterie-Regiment Nr 129	Yellow	Tombak	-	XVII

Generalfeldmarfchall von Hindenburg
Chef des Generalstabes des Feldheeres. Neueste Aufnahme nach dem Leben.
7772
Verlag Gust. Liersch & Co., Berlin S.W. ·   A. Kühlewindt Hofphotograph Königsberg Pr.

Generalfeldmarschall Paul von Hindenburg, wearing the 1910 field grey and the Pour Le Mérite. Born at Posen in 1847 Hindenburg was a veteran of the 1866 victory over Austria at Könnigratz and of the Franco-Prussian War. Called out of retirement, his remarkable performance on the Eastern Front in command of Eighth Army propelled him to unexpected fame and he was presented with the Pour Le Mérite (Blue Max) on 2 September 1914. In 1916 he would be promoted to Chief of General Staff. The general's greatcoat shown here had scarlet facings.

Men of Reserve Hussar Regiment Nr 6 wearing the field grey Atilla with grey loops and in one instance simplified cuffs. The headgear is the *Pelzmütze* with cover; note that the field sign is worn exposed and that the chin strap can be either inside or outside the busby covers, which bear the inscription 'R 6'. Carbines are carried and small cavalry type ammunition pouches are worn. IWM Q114135.

1. Lothringisches Infanterie-Regiment Nr 130	Yellow	Tombak	–	XVI
2. Lothringisches Infanterie-Regiment Nr 131	L. Green	Tombak	–	XXI
1. Unter-Elsässisches Infanterie-Regiment Nr 132	Red	Tombak	–	XV
3. Lothringisches Infanterie-Regiment Nr 135	Yellow	Tombak	–	XVI
4. Lothringisches Infanterie-Regiment Nr 136	Red	Tombak	–	XV
2. Unter-Elsässisches Infanterie-Regiment Nr 137	L. Green	Tombak	–	XXI
3. Unter-Elsässisches Infanterie-Regiment Nr 138	L. Green	Tombak	–	XXI
4. Westpreußisches Infanterie-Regiment Nr 140	White	Tombak	–	II

Men of 4th company, *Ersatz* battalion, Reserve Infantry
Regiment Nr 55, pictured at Cologne in December 1914. The
1910 field grey uniform is worn with obsolete ammunition
pouches and plain grey Pickelhaube covers. SB.

Kulmer Infanterie-Regiment Nr 141	Yellow	Tombak	-	XVII
7. Badisches Infanterie-Regiment Nr 142	Yellow	Tombak	-	XIV
4. Unter-Elsässisches Infanterie-Regiment Nr 143	Red	Tombak	-	XV
5. Lothringisches Infanterie-Regiment Nr 144	Yellow	Tombak	-	XVI
Königs-Infanterie-Regiment 6. Lothringisches Nr 145	L. Blue	Tombak	-	XVI
1. Masurisches Infanterie-Regiment Nr 146	L. Blue	Tombak	-	XX
2. Masurisches Infanterie-Regiment Nr 147	L. Blue	Tombak	-	XX
5. Westpreußisches Infanterie-Regiment Nr 148	L. Blue	Tombak	-	XX
6. Westpreußisches Infanterie-Regiment Nr 149	White	Tombak	-	II
1. Ermländisches Infanterie-Regiment Nr 150	L. Blue	Tombak	-	XX
2. Ermländisches Infanterie-Regiment Nr 151	L. Blue	Tombak	-	XX

Deutch Ordens-Infanterie-Regiment Nr 152	Red	Tombak	-	XX
8. Thüringisches Infanterie-Regiment Nr 153	Red	Tombak	-	IV
5. Niederschlesisches Infanterie-Regiment Nr 154	Yellow	Tombak	-	V
7. Westpreußisches Infanterie-Regiment Nr 155	Yellow	Tombak	-	V
3. Schlesiches Infanterie-Regiment Nr 156	Yellow	Tombak	-	VI
4. Schlesiches Infanterie-Regiment Nr 157	Yellow	Tombak	-	VI
7. Lothringisches Infanterie-Regiment Nr 158	L. Blue	Tombak	-	VII
8. Lothringisches Infanterie-Regiment Nr 159	L. Blue	Tombak	-	VII
9. Rheinisches Infanterie-Regiment Nr 160	L. Blue	Tombak	-	VIII
10. Rheinisches Infanterie-Regiment Nr 161	L. Blue	Tombak	-	VIII
Infanterie-Regiment Lübeck (3. Hanseatisches) Nr 162	White	Tombak	-	IX
Schleswig-Holsteinsches Infanterie-Regiment Nr 163	White	Tombak	-	IX
4. Hannoversches Infanterie-Regiment Nr 164	White	Tombak	-	X
5. Hannoversches Infanterie-Regiment Nr 165	Red	Tombak	-	IV
Infanterie-Regiment Hessen-Homburg Nr 166	L. Green	Tombak	-	XXI
1. Ober-Elsässisches Infanterie Regiment Nr 167	Red	Tombak	-	XI
5. Großherzoglich Hessisches Infanterie-Regiment Nr 168	Red	Tombak	-	XVIII
8. Badisches Infanterie-Regiment Nr 169	Red	Tombak	-	XIV
9. Badisches Infanterie-Regiment Nr 170	L. Blue	Tombak	-	XIV
2. Ober-Elsässisches Infanterie-Regiment Nr 171	Red	Tombak	-	XV
3. Ober-Elsässisches Infanterie Regiment Nr 172	Red	Tombak	-	XV
9. Lothringisches Infanterie-Regiment Nr 173	Yellow	Tombak	-	XVI

Other differences: most of these regiments had their number on the shoulder strap; exceptions which had monograms or cyphers were regiments 34, 47, 53, 72, 80, 86, 88, 89, 90, 91, 92, 93, 94, 95, 109, 110, 111, 114, 115, 116, 117, 144 and 153. Brandenburg cuffs were worn by all the above except regiment 109 which had Swedish cuffs. All jacket and collar piping was scarlet. Hanoverian regiments 73 and 79 wore the yellow on light blue cuff title 'GIBRALTAR' on the right arm. Regiments 73, 74, 77, 78, 164 and 165 all carried a 'WATERLOO' battle honour on the helmet plate, and regiment 73 additionally carried the honour 'PENINSULA'. Regiments 25, 80, 86 and 145 were entitled to the use of the parade plume on the *Pickelhaube* in full dress. Double *Litzen* were worn by regiments 89, 109 and 115: Old Prussian *Litzen* were worn by number 90. The *Litzen* of regiment 80 lacked the usual red centre line. Whilst the majority used the Prussian state cockade regiments 55, 71, 75, 83, 89, 90, 91, 92, 93, 94, 96, 109-118, 142, 153, 162, 169 and 170 all kept their own distinctive state cockades on the *Pickelhaube*. Regiments 89, 90, 109-118, 142, 168, 169

Dressing station: Eastern Front, 1916.

The sentries in the left foreground are drawn from three different units. Underneath the dressing station sign is a private soldier of the *Infanterie-Regiment von der Golz (7. Pommersches) Nr 54.* This unit was a part of 36th Reserve Division, which occupied the Friedrichstadt sector south east of Riga from late 1915; being moved to Galicia in the autumn of 1916 and committed to action against the Russians East of Brzezany during October. The man depicted is wearing the usual infantry uniform with Brandenburg cuffs and *Feldmütze* with scarlet band. Extra protection from the elements is provided by a toque or sleeve of cloth over the head and a pair of light grey canvas waterproof over-trousers. The heavily bearded *Landsturm* infantryman is equipped in typically obsolete style with the G 88 rifle and battered 1860 type shako, lacking its badge. The non regulation fur lined brown leather overcoat worn over an issue greatcoat, gloves and massive felt over-boots were useful in cold weather. The pipe smoking *Jäger* has a cap of grey green material with a green band: his greatcoat is of the 1901 type with integral hood stored in the collar. He carries not only ammunition pouches and entrenching tool, but the distinctive green bayonet knot of the

Jäger. The officer approaching along the track is wearing the grey double-breasted officers' greatcoat, riding boots, and soft peaked cap with the usual black band and scarlet piping of an artillery unit.

In the background, stretcher bearers unload wounded men from an ambulance. Medical services were organised so that each battalion of the army had two medical officers, four medical NCOs, and 16 stretcher bearers who were counted as non-combatants and wore Red Cross brassards. In the front line each company maintained a small aid post but the main regimental *Truppenverbandplatz,* or troop dressing station, manned by three officers and eight stretcher bearers, was held further back. Transport provision for the seriously wounded to field hospitals was maintained by the *Sanitätskompagnie,* or bearer company, of each division. These bearer companies would establish other facilities in the course of their work including the *Wagenhalteplatz* or ambulance station; a main dressing station or *Hauptverbandplatz*; and a collecting station for the lightly wounded known as the *Lichterverwunden-Sammelplatz.* The wounded themselves were identified by a series of labels as 'walking'; 'able to be transported'; or 'not able to be transported'. Painting by Christa Hook.

and 170 likewise kept their own state helmet plate. The belt buckle motto for Prussia and the smaller states was 'GOTT MIT UNS'. The Hessian belt plate had a crown but no motto.

Saxon Regiments, *Königlich Sächsisches*

1. (Leib-) Grenadier-Regiment Nr 100	White	Tombak	White	XII
2. Grenadier-Regiment Nr 101 Kaiser Wilhelm	White	Tombak	White	XII
3. Infanterie-Regiment Nr 102 König Ludwig III. von Bayern	White	Tombak	-	XII
4. Infanterie-Regiment Nr 103	White	Tombak	-	XII
5. Infanterie-Regiment Kronprinz Nr 104	Red	Tombak	-	XIX
6. Infanterie-Regiment Nr 105 König Wilhelm II. von Württemberg	Red	Tombak	-	XV
7. Infanterie-Regiment König Georg Nr 106	Red	Tombak	-	XIX
8. Infanterie-Regiment Prinz Johann Georg Nr 107	Red	Tombak	-	XIX
9. Infanterie-Regiment Nr 133	Red	Tombak	-	XIX
10. Infanterie-Regiment Nr 134	Red	Tombak	-	XIX

Officers and NCOs around the Christmas tree at Lorgies, Western Front, 1914. At least two of the officers are wearing the *Litewka* or double-breasted undress jacket with collar patches. SB.

11. Infanterie-Regiment Nr 139	Red	Tombak	-	XIX
12. Infanterie-Regiment Nr 177	White	Tombak	-	XII
13. Infanterie-Regiment Nr 178	White	Tombak	-	XII
14. Infanterie-Regiment Nr 179	Red	Tombak	-	XIX
15. Infanterie-Regiment Nr 181	Red	Tombak	-	XIX
16. Infanterie-Regiment Nr 182	White	Tombak	-	XII

Other differences: Saxon troops maintained their separate identity by means of a *Waffenrock* with two, rather than four, buttons on the rear skirt ornamentation, and a cuff which had two buttons one above and one below the piping. The collar, cuff, and *Waffenrock* front pipings were all scarlet. The elite regiments 100 and 101 were exceptional in wearing the Swedish style cuff and double *Litzen* with a red centre line. They were also entitled to the black parade plume for ceremonial. Saxon troops wore the state helmet plate, the white, green, white, state cockade and distinctive belt plate with the motto 'PROVIDENTIAE MEMOR'. Regiments 100,101, 104 and 106 wore cyphers on their shoulder straps, the rest their number in the national sequence, i.e. 102, 103, etc.

<u>Württemberg Regiments;</u> *Königlich Württembergisches*

Grenadier-Regiment Königin Olga (1. Württembergisches) Nr 119	Red	Tombak	White	XIII
Infanterie-Regiment Kaiser Wilhelm, König von Preußen (2. Württembergisches) Nr 120	Red	Tombak	-	XIII
Infanterie-Regiment Alt-Württemberg (3. Württembergisches) Nr 121	Red	Tombak	-	XIII
Füsilier-Regiment Kaiser Franz Joseph von Österreich, König von Ungarn (4. Württembergisches) Nr 122	Red	Tombak	-	XIII
Grenadier-Regiment König Karl (5. Württembergisches) Nr 123	Red	Tombak	White	XIII
Infanterie-Regiment König Wilhelm I (6. Württembergisches) Nr 124	Red	Tombak	-	XIII
Infanterie-Regiment Kaiser Friedrich, König von Preußen (7. Württembergisches) Nr 125	Red	Tombak	-	XIII
8. Württembergisches Infanterie-Regiment Nr 126 Großherzog Freidrich von Baden	Red	Tombak	-	XV
9. Württembergisches Infanterie-Regiment Nr 127	Red	Tombak	-	XIII
10. Württembergisches Infanterie-Regiment Nr 180	Red	Tombak	-	XIII

Other differences: Württemberg regiments could be recognised by their state helmet plate; black, red, black state cockade; and belt buckle with motto 'FURCHTLOS UND TREU'. The *Litzen* worn by regiments 119 and 123 were double with red centre line. Black parade plumes were used by regiments120 and 123, whilst III Battalion of the 119 wore the white. In 1914 Württemberg regiments wore Brandenburg cuffs with the exception of regiments 119 and 123 which wore Swedish cuffs. Interestingly Swedish cuffs were also worn by some Württemberg regiments raised at, and after, the outbreak of war. National numbers in red were worn on the shoulder straps except by regiments 119, 120, 123, 124 and 125 which wore cyphers. As usual, scarlet piping edged the collar, cuffs and front of the Waffenrock.

<u>Bavarian Regiments:</u> *Königlich Bayerisches*

Infanterie-Leib-Regiment	White	Nickel	White	Bav I
1. Infanterie-Regiment-König	White	Tombak	-	Bav I
2. Infanterie-Regiment-Kronprinz	White	Tombak	-	Bav I
3. Infanterie-Regiment Prinz Karl von Bayern	White	Tombak	-	Bav I
4. Infanterie-Regiment König Wilhelm von Württemberg	Red	Tombak	-	Bav II
5. Infanterie-Regiment Großherzog Ernst Ludwig von Hessen	Red	Tombak	-	Bav II

6. Infanterie-Regiment Kaiser Wilhelm König von Preußen	Yellow	Tombak	-	Bav III
7. Infanterie-Regiment Prinz Leopold	Yellow	Tombak	-	Bav III
8. Infanterie-Regiment Großherzog Friedrich II von Baden	Red	Tombak	-	Bav II
9. Infanterie-Regiment Wrede	Red	Tombak	-	Bav II
10. Infanterie-Regiment König	Yellow	Tombak	-	Bav III
11. Infanterie-Regiment von der Tann	Yellow	Tombak	-	Bav III
12. Infanterie-Regiment Prinz Arnulf	White	Tombak	-	Bav I
13. Infanterie-Regiment Franz Joseph I., Kaiser von Osterreich und Apostolisher König von Ungarn	Yellow	Tombak	-	Bav III
14. Infanterie-Regiment Hartmann	Yellow	Tombak	-	Bav III
15. Infanterie-Regiment König Friedrich August von Sachsen	White	Tombak	-	Bav I
16. Infanterie-Regiment Großherzog Ferdinand von Toscana	Red	Tombak	-	Bav II
17. Infanterie-Regiment Orff	Yellow	Tombak	-	Bav III
18. Infanterie-Regiment Prinz Ludwig Ferdinand	Red	Tombak	-	Bav II
19. Infanterie-Regiment König Viktor Emanuel III. von Italien	Yellow	Tombak	-	Bav III
20. Infanterie-Regiment Prinz Franz.	White	Tombak	-	Bav I
21. Infanterie-Regiment Großherzog Friedrich Franz IV. von Mecklenburg-Schwerin	Yellow	Tombak	-	Bav III
22. Infanterie-Regiment Fürst Wilhelm von Hohenzollern	Red	Tombak	-	Bav II
23. Infanterie-Regiment König Ferdinand der Bulgaren	Red	Tombak	-	Bav II

Other differences: Bavarian units maintained their own local number of precedence separate from the regimental number system operating in the other states. Thus it was that though Bavarian regiments 1,2,3, 6, 10 and the *Leib* regiment wore cyphers on their shoulder straps, the others wore numerals in red up to 23, so duplicating some of the numbers in use by Prussian units. All were grouped into three distinct Corps Districts numbered I, II and III. Bavarian units wore their state helmet plate, and a white, light blue, white cockade. On the belt appeared the motto 'IN TREUE FEST'. The *Leib* regiment was further distinguished by its white metal helmet plate, double *Litzen* and Swedish cuffs. Scarlet piping appeared on the collar, cuffs, and *Waffenrock* front of all regiments; the Bavarian button was distinguished by its lion motif.

Jäger and *Schützen*

Garde-Jäger-Bataillon	Green	Tombak	Yellow	Garde

A selection of shoulder straps of both the 1910 and 1915
types. The majority are of numbered infantry, or Reserve
infantry, regiments. There are both piped and war economy
unpiped examples. A few are worthy of further comment.
Bottom left is the strap of Fusilier regiment Nr 80 with its
distinctive cypher; top row second from right, is the grey green
strap of *Schützen* regiment Nr 108; bottom right is a 1915 type
Foot Artillery strap. Queen's Lancashire Regiment.

Garde-Schützen-Bataillon	Green	Tombak	Yellow	Garde
Jäger-Bataillon Graf Yorck von Wartenburg (Ostpreußisches) Nr 1	Green	Tombak	-	XX
Jäger-Bataillon Fürst Bismarck (Pommersches) Nr 2	Green	Tombak	-	XVII
Brandenburgisches Jäger-Bataillon Nr 3	Green	Tombak	-	III
Magdeburgisches Jäger-Bataillon Nr 4	Green	Tombak	-	IV
Jäger-Bataillon von Neumann (1. Schlesisches) Nr 5	Green	Tombak	-	V
2. Schlesisches Jäger-Bataillon Nr 6	Green	Tombak	-	VI
Westfälisches Jäger-Bataillon Nr 7	Green	Tombak	-	VII

Landsturm at Munchengladbach, 1914. Note the obsolete shakos, musicians shoulder 'wings' and G88 rifles.

Rheinisches Jäger-Bataillon Nr 8	Green	Tombak	-	XV
Lauenburgisches Jäger-Bataillon Nr 9	Green	Tombak	-	IX
Hannoversches Jäger-Bataillon Nr 10	Green	Tombak	-	IX
Kurhessisches Jäger-Bataillon Nr 11	Green	Tombak	-	XI

Saxon *Jäger* and *Schützen*

1. Jäger-Bataillon Nr 12	Green	Nickel	-	XII
2. Jäger-Bataillon Nr 13	Green	Nickel	-	XII
Schützen-(Füsilier-) Regiment Prinz Georg Nr 108	Green	Tombak	-	XII

Mecklenburg *Jäger*

Großherzoglich Mecklenburgisches Jäger Bataillon Nr 14	Green	Tombak	White	XV

Bavarian *Jäger*

1. Jäger-Bataillon Prinz Ludwig	Green	Tombak	-	Bav I
2. Jäger-Bataillon	Green	Tombak	-	Bav II

Other differences: *Jäger* and *Schützen* wore the grey-green version of the *Waffenrock*, except Bavarian *Jäger* who wore field grey. Jacket pipings were green, except in the case of the collars and cuffs of the *Garde Schützen* and *Schützen Regiment 108* which were black. The shoulder straps of the *Garde* had no insignia: most other units displayed red numerals, but the Bavarians had the battalion number in green. Saxon units had a red hunting horn in addition to their red numerals. Swedish cuffs were worn by all units except the *Garde Schützen* who wore French cuffs with three vertical buttons and *Litzen* to match. Shakos were worn with front and rear peaks by all units except the Saxons whose hats had front peaks only. State belt plates matched the area of origin. *Garde* star shako plates were worn by the *Garde*; Grenadier eagles with the 'FWR' cypher were worn by Prussian battalions 1,2,5 and 6; line eagles by 3,4,8, 9 and 11. *Jäger Battalion 10* was distinguished by the eagle with 'WATERLOO', 'PENINSULA', and 'VENTA DEL POZO' battle honours and 'GIBRALTAR' cuff title. The Mecklenburg, Bavarian, and Saxon units had helmet plates with their respective state arms. State 'field signs' were likewise worn atop the shako by all but the Saxons with *Battalion 7* having the white, red, blue cockade of Schaumburg-Lippe, and Mecklenburg *Battalion 14* having quartered carmine and blue with a yellow cross. The *Litzen* were of the double variety with a green centre line for the *Garde Jäger* and *Battalion 14*, and black for the *Garde Schützen*.

Maschinengewehr-Abteilungen; 'Machine-gun Detachments'

Garde-Maschinengewehr-Abteilung Nr 1	Red	Tombak	Yellow	Garde
Garde-Maschinengewehr-Abteilung Nr 2	Red	Tombak	Yellow	Garde
Maschinengewehr-Abteilung Nr 1	Red	Tombak	-	VI
Maschinengewehr-Abteilung Nr 2	Red	Tombak	-	VIII
Maschinengewehr-Abteilung Nr 3	Red	Tombak	-	XXI
Maschinengewehr-Abteilung Nr 4	Red	Tombak	-	XVII
Maschinengewehr-Abteilung Nr 5	Red	Tombak	-	I
Maschinengewehr-Abteilung Nr 6	Red	Tombak	-	XVI
Maschinengewehr-Abteilung Nr 7	Red	Tombak	-	XVI
(Königlich Sächsische) Maschinengewehr-Abteilung Nr 8	Red	Tombak	-	XIX
Königlich Bayerische Maschinengewehr-Abteilung Nr 1	L. Green	Tombak	-	Bav II

Other distinctions: the machine-gun detachments wore a grey-green *Jäger* style uniform with scarlet piping and Swedish cuffs, the headgear being a shako in grey-green cloth with tan brown leather top, peaks and reinforcement. The *Garde* shoulder straps were plain, whilst the line were numbered 1 to 8, with the numeral 1 repeated for the Bavarian detachment. The *Garde* wore the *Garde* star shako plate in silver, and double yellow *Litzen* on the collar; the *Litzen* of the 1 *Garde* had a red infill in between the two sets of lace, the 2 *Garde* black. 2 *Garde* were further differentiated by green piping to their *Waffenrock*, with black piping at collar and cuff. Line detachments 1–7 wore the Prussian eagle shako plate and the Saxons and

Bavarians their state variations and cockades. These 11 machine-gun detachments were attached to the cavalry on mobilisation: infantry regiments already had their own machine-gun companies. It should be noted that 15 'Fortress' or *Festungs* machine-gun detachments also existed on the outbreak of war having been raised in 1913 and attached to the

infantry. The majority of these were part of XVI or XVII Corps districts. Many 'Machine-Gun Sharpshooter' and *Musketen* units were raised as the war progressed.

CAVALRY
<u>*Kürassiere* and *Schwere Reiter*</u>: the Cuirassier and Heavy Horse

	Pipings	Buttons	Litzen	Corps
Regiment der Gardes du Corps	Scarlet	Nickel	White	Garde
Garde Kürassiere Regiment	Cornflower	Nickel	White	Garde
Leib-Kürassiere Regiment Großer Kurfürst (Schlesisches) Nr 1	Black	Tombak	-	VI
Kürassiere-Regiment Königin (Pommersches) Nr 2	Crimson	Nickel	-	II
Kürassiere-Regiment Graf Wrangel (Ostpreußisches) Nr 3	L. Blue	Nickel	-	I
Kürassiere-Regiment von Driessen (Westfälisches) Nr 4	Scarlet	Nickel	-	VII
Kürassiere-Regiment Herzog Friedrich Eugen von Württemberg (Westpreußisches) Nr 5	Pink	Tombak	-	XX
Kürassiere-Regiment Kaiser Nikolaus I. von Rußland (Brandenburgisches) Nr 6	Blue	Tombak	-	III
Kürassiere-Regiment von Seydlitz (Magdeburgisches) Nr 7	Yellow	Nickel	-	IV
Kürassiere-Regiment Geßler(Rheinisches) Nr 8	L. Green	Tombak	-	VIII
(Königlich Sächsisches) Garde Reiter Regiment	Cornflower	Tombak	-	XII
(Königlich Sächsisches) Karabiner Regiment	Cornflower	Tombak	-	XIX
1. (Königlich Bayerisches) Schweres Reiter-Regiment Prinz Karl von Bayern	Scarlet	Nickel	-	Bav I
2. (Königlich Bayerisches) Schweres Reiter-Regiment Erzherzog Franz Ferdinand von Österreich-Este	Scarlet	Tombak	-	Bav I

Other distinctions: the jacket was of a special pattern with a stand up collar, Swedish cuffs and regimental pattern lace or *Bortenbesatz* to both collar and cuffs. The regimental piping colours noted above applied not only to the outer edge of the shoulder straps but also to the jacket front, rear, bottom edge and cuffs. On the shoulder straps a white line ran inside the regimental piping. The Prussian *Garde Kürassiere*, the Saxon *Karabiner* and the Bavarian *Reiter* shoulder straps had no cypher or numeral. Regiments 1, 2, 6, 8 and the Saxon *Garde* had scarlet regimental cyphers, others had scarlet numerals. The *Litzen* of the *Garde du Corps* had a red centre line, that of the *Garde-Kürassiere* was cornflower blue. With the exception of

Mess tin, water bottle, and 1911 type grey canvas *Zeltbahn*.
(King's Liverpool Regiment: National Museums and Galleries on Merseyside)

the Bavarian units, which wore a black leather *Pickelhaube* in the dragoon style, other *Kürassiere* and *Schwere Reiter* wore a distinctive polished metal lobster tailed Curassier helmet with a spike and the relevant cockades. For the Saxons this helmet was in Tombak, with a silver star on which appeared the Saxon arms in

'Dragonen': Dragoons

Tombak. Most of the Prussian *Kürassiere* had polished steel helmets with an eagle plate, but both the *Garde* regiments and Nr 6 used Tombak helmets. The *Garde* had *Garde* star helmet plates in silver and, most remarkably, wore a metal flying eagle atop their helmets when on parade. The helmet of the *Leib* Regiment was distinguished by the motto 'PRO GLORIA ET PATRIA', that of the Pommeranian *Königin Regiment Nr 2* by the honour 'HOHENFRIEDBERG 4. JUNI 1745'.

	Piping	Buttons	Litzen	Corps
1. Garde-Dragoner Regiment *Königin Victoria von Goßbritannien und Irland*	Red	Tombak	Yellow	Garde
2. Garde-Dragoner Regiment *Kaiserin Alexandra von Rußland*	Red	Nickel	White	Garde
Dragoner Regiment Prinz *Albrecht von Preußen (Litthauisches) Nr 1*	Red	Tombak	-	I
1. Brandeburgisches Dragoner Regiment Nr 2	Black	Tombak	-	III

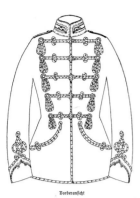

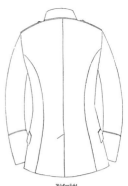

Der Attila für die Offiziere der Preußischen Husaren-Regimenter (ausschließlich Leib-Garde-Husaren-R.)

Vorderansicht

Rückansicht

Der kleine Rock für Offiziere und obere Beamte
(Für die Offiziere und oberen Beamten der Bayerischen Armee mit blau-silberner Hoheitsborde um den Kragen)

Vorderansicht

Rückansicht

Vorderansicht

Rückansicht

Die Bluse
Einheitliches Bekleidungsstück für den Felddienst für Offiziere und Mannschaften der Armee
(Für die Bayerischen Truppen blau-silber bezw. blau-weiße Hoheitsborde um den Kragen)

Vorderansicht

Rückansicht

Der Waffenrock der Garde-Infanterie (für Linien-Infanterie Kragen ohne Litze, vorn abgerundet)
Desgl. der Garde-Dragoner, Garde-Jäger, Garde-Schützen, Garde-Pioniere, Garde-Verkehrstruppen,
Garde-Train, Garde-Artillerie und Krankenwärter des Gardekorps

Line drawings of the various jackets sanctioned by the 1915 regulations. From top left: the hussar Attila; the *Kleine Rock* or officers undress *Litewka*; the *Bluse* for field service; and the new field grey dress *Waffenrock*.

Grenadiere Regiment zu Pferde Freiherr von Derflinger (Neumärk) Nr 3	Pink	Nickel	-	II
Dragoner Regiment von Bredow (1. Schlesisiches) Nr 4	L. Yellow	Nickel	-	V
Dragoner Regiment Freiherr von Manteuffel (Rheinisches) Nr 5	Red	Nickel	-	XI
Magdeburgisches Dragoner Regiment Nr 6	Black	Nickel	-	XVIII
Westfälisches Dragoner Regiment Nr 7	Pink	Tombak	-	XXI
Dragoner Regiment König Freidrich III (2. Schlesisches) Nr 8	Yellow	Tombak	-	VI
Dragoner Regiment König Karl I von Rumänien (1. Hannoversches) Nr 9	White	Tombak	-	XVI
Dragoner Regiment König Albert von Sachsen (Ostpreusiches) Nr 10	White	Nickel	-	XX

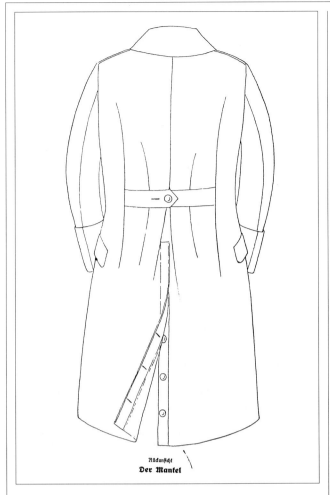

Schematic rear view of the 1915 greatcoat or *Mantel*.

An unusual picture showing what appears to be an old woman wearing an NCOs 1915 model greatcoat, felt *Ersatz* Prussian *Pickelhaube* and sword with knot. SB.

Dragoner Regiment von Wedel (Pommersches) Nr 11	Crimson	Tombak	-	XX
Dragoner Regiment von Arnim (2. Brandenburgisches) Nr 12	Crimson	Nickel	-	II
Schleswig - Holsteinsches Dragoner Regiment Nr 13	Red	Tombak	-	XVI
Kürmark Dragoner Regiment Nr 14	Black	Tombak	-	XV
3. Schlesisches Dragoner Regiment Nr 15	Pink	Nickel	-	XV
2. Hannoversches Dragoner Regiment Nr 16	Yellow	Nickel	-	X
1. Großherzoglich Mecklenburgisches Dragoner Regiment Nr 17	Red	Tombak	-	IX
2. Großherzoglich Mecklenburgisches Dragoner Regiment Nr 18	Black	Nickel	-	IX
Oldenburgisches Dragoner Regiment Nr 19	White	Nickel	-	X
Baden Leib-Dragoner Regiment Nr 20	Red	Nickel	-	XIV

Baden Dragoner Regiment Nr 21	Yellow	Nickel	-	XIV
Baden Dragoner Regiment Nr 22	Black	Nickel	-	XIV
Garde-Dragoner Regiment (1. Großherzoglich Hessisches Nr 23)	Red	Nickel	White	XVII
Leib-Dragoner Regiment (2. Großherzoglich Hessisches Nr 24)	White	Nickel	-	XVII
Dragoner Regiment Königin Olga (1. Württembergisches) Nr 25	White	Tombak	White	XIII
Dragoner Regiment König (2. Württembergisches) Nr 26	Yellow	Nickel	-	XIII

Other distinctions: Dragoons wore infantry style jackets but with Swedish cuffs and standing collars rounded off at the front. The headgear was a *Pickelhaube* with square cut peak. The Prussian guard dragoons wore the guard eagle on their *Pickelhaube*, yellow metal with white metal star for the first, and all white metal for the second. The *Haarbusch* for both guard regiments was white. Dragoon regiment Nr 1, and Grenadier regiment Nr 3 used the guard style eagle, but without the star. From 1861 the cap of regiment Nr 2 featured a small eagle between the cockades. The eagle of regiment Nr 9 featured the Hanoverian honours PENINSULA, WATERLOO, and GÖHRDE; regiment Nr 16 had WATERLOO only. The headgear of the minor states bore the appropriate state arms and cockades. The cuff and collar pipings of regiments 13 to 16 were white. The guards and regiments 3, 8, 9, 10, 17, 18, 23, 24, 25 and 26 all had cyphers rather than numbers on their shoulder straps, and both numerals and cyphers were in red.

Die Bayerischen Chevaulegers: the Bavarian Light Horse

	Piping	Buttons	Corps
1. Chevauleger Regiment Kaiser Nikolaus von Rußland	Crimson	Tombak	Bav III
2. Chevauleger Regiment Taxis	Crimson	Nickel	Bav III
3. Chevauleger Regiment Herzog Karl Theodor	Peach red	Tombak	Bav II
4. Chevauleger Regiment König	Red	Nickel	Bav I
5. Chevauleger Regiment Erzherzog Friedrich vonÖsterreich	Red	Tombak	Bav II
6. Chevauleger Regiment Prinz Albrecht von Preußen	Peach red	Nickel	Bav III
7. Chevauleger Regiment Prinz Alfons	White	Tombak	Bav III
8. Chevauleger Regiment	White	Nickel	Bav I

Other distinctions: the jacket of the Bavarian Light Horse was similar to that of the Ulan, but had Swedish cuffs, a stand and fall collar, shoulder straps with piping and no *Litzen* were worn. The formal headgear was a *Pickelhaube* with the Bavarian arms and cockades.

Husaren: Hussars	Regimental colour	Cord Twist	Corps
Leib-Garde-Husaren Regiment	Scarlet	Yellow	Garde
1 Leib-Husaren Regiment Nr 1	Black	White	XVII
2 Leib-Husaren-Regiment 'Königin Viktoria von Preussen' Nr 2	Black	White	XVII
Husaren-Regiment 'von Zeiten' (Brandenburgisches) Nr 3	Scarlet	White	III
Husaren-Regiment 'von Schill' (1 Schlesisches) Nr 4	Brown	Yellow	VI
Husaren-Regiment 'Fürst Blücher von Wahlstatt' (Pommersches Nr 5)	Madder Red	White	XVII
Husaren-Regiment 'Graf Goetzen' (2 Schlesisches) Nr 6	Green	Yellow	VI
Husaren-Regiment 'König Wilhelm I' (1 Rheinisches) Nr 7	Russian Blue	Yellow	VIII
Husaren-Regiment 'Kaiser Nikolaus II von Rußland' (1 Westfälisches) Nr 8	Blue	White	VII
2 Rheinisches Husaren-Regiment Nr 9	Cornflower Blue	Yellow	XV
Magdeburgisches Husaren-Regiment Nr 10	Green	Yellow	IV
2 Westfälisches Husaren-Regiment Nr 11	Green	White	VII
Thüringisches Husaren-Regiment Nr 12	Cornflower Blue	White	IV
Husaren-Regiment 'König Humbert von Italien' (1 Kurhessisches) Nr 13	Cornflower Blue	White	XVI
Husaren-Regiment 'Landgraf Freidrich II von Hessen-Homburg' (2 Kurhessisches) Nr 14	Blue	White	XI
Husaren-Regiment 'Königin Wilhelmina der Niederlande' (Hannoversches) Nr 15	Blue	White	XI
Husaren-Regiment 'Kaiser Franz Joseph von Österreich, König von Ungarn' (Schleswig-Holsteinisches) Nr 16	Cornflower Blue	White	IX
Braunschweigisches Husaren-Regiment Nr 17	Black	Yellow	X
1 Sächsisches Husaren-Regiment ' König Albert' Nr 18	Cornflower Blue	Yellow	XII

2 Sächsisches-Husaren-Regiment 'Kronprinz Wilhelm des Deutschen Reiches und von Preussen'Nr 19	Cornflower Blue	White	XIX
3 Sächsisches Husaren-Regiment Nr 20	Cornflower Blue	White	XII

Other distinctions: Hussars wore the *Pelzmütze* or busby, and a field grey service version of the old Attila, with grey loops but coloured shoulder cords. These distinctive cords were a mixture of the regimental colour twisted together with the colour of the old full dress jacket loops, and bore the regimental number or cypher (for example, Hussar Regiment Nr 6 had shoulder cords of green and yellow, with the number). For field grey caps bands were of the regimental colour. The death's head was worn on the caps of the 1 and 2 *Leib-Husaren*, and Regiment Nr 17. Regiment Nr 20 was only raised in 1910, and only ever wore the field grey Atilla. Greatcoat collar patches were Black for *Leib-Husaren* Nr 2; yellow for Nr 4, 15, and 16; madder red for Nr 5; cornflower blue for Nr 8, 9 and 12; pompadour red for Nr 10; crimson for Nr 19; and field grey with cornflower blue piping for Nr 20. The collar patches of the remainder were red. Greatcoat shoulder straps were red for the *Garde Leib-Husaren*, and Nr 17; black for Nr 1 and 2; blue for Nr 3, 8, 14 and 15; brown for Nr 4; madder for Nr 5; green for Nr 6, 10 and 11; Russian blue for Nr 7; cornflower blue for Nr 9, 12, 13, 16, 18 and 19; and field grey for Nr 20. The Saxon regiments had squared off rather than pointed greatcoat shoulder straps and were piped: yellow for Nr 18, white for Nr 19 and 20.

Ulanen: Lancers

	Regimental Piping	Litzen	Corps
1 Garde Ulanen-Regiment	White	White	Garde
2 Garde Ulanen-Regiment	Red	Yellow	Garde
3 Garde Ulanen-Regiment	Yellow	White	Garde
Ulanen-Regiment Kaiser Alexander III von Rußland (Westpreußisches) Nr 1	White	-	V
Ulanen-Regiment von Katzler (Schlesisches) Nr 2	Red	-	VI
Ulanen-Regiment Kaiser Alexander II von Rußland (Brandenburgisches) Nr 3	Yellow	-	III
Ulanen-Regiment von Schmidt (Pommersches) Nr 4	Light Blue	-	XX
Westfälisches Ulanen-Regiment Nr 5	White	-	VII
Thüringisches Ulanen-Regiment Nr 6	Red	-	XVIII
Ulanen-Regiment Großherzog Friedrich von Baden (Rheinisches) Nr 7	Yellow	-	XXI
Ulanen-Regiment Graf zu Dohna (Ostpreußisches) Nr 8	Light Blue	-	I
2 Pommersches Ulanen-Regiment Nr 9	White	-	II
Ulanen-Regiment Prinz August von Württemberg (Posensches) Nr 10	Crimson	-	V

Freikorps **soldiers in Berlin during the post-war revolution.**
Although the Erhardt armoured car and flamethrower demand
attention some of the soldiers are wearing the peakless
'Turkish' or Ottoman contract variant of the Model 1918 steel
helmet. TRH Pictures.

Ulanen-Regiment Graf Haeseler (2.Brandenburgisches) Nr 11	Yellow	-	XXI
Litthauishes Ulanen-Regiment Nr 12	Light Blue	-	I
Königs Ulanen-Regiment (1 Hannoversches) Nr 13	White	-	X
2 Hannoversches Ulanen-Regiment Nr 14	Crimson	-	VXI
Schleswig-Holsteinsches Ulanen-Regiment Nr 15	Yellow	-	XXI
Ulanen-Regiment Hennigs von Treffenfeld (Altmark) Nr 16	Light blue	-	IV
1. Königlich Sächsisches Ulanen-Regiment Nr 17 Kaiser Franz Joseph von Österreich König von Ungarn	White	-	XII
2. Königlich Sächsisches Ulanen-Regiment Nr 18	Red	-	XIX
Ulanen-Regiment König Karl (1. Württembergisches) Nr 19	Red	-	XIII

Ulanen-Regiment König Wilhelm I (2. Württembergisches) Nr 20	Yellow	-	XIII
3. Königlich Sächsisches Ulanen-Regiment Nr 21 Kaiser Wilhelm König von Preußen	Yellow	-	XIX
1. (Königlich Bayerisches) Ulanen-Regiment Kaiser Wilhelm II König von Preußen	Crimson	-	Bav II
2. (Königlich Bayerisches) Ulanen-Regiment König	Crimson	-	Bav II

Other distinctions: *Ulanen* wore the *Ulanka* jacket with plastron front and stand up collar. The regimentally coloured pipings ran around the cuffs, shoulder straps, collar, jacket front, down the back, and around the rear skirt ornaments. Most units wore pear shaped shoulder straps, with regiments Nr 1, 3, 6, 13, 16, 19 and 20 having red cyphers, the others red numerals. The Saxon regiments had square topped shoulder straps; the Bavarians had stand and fall collars. Guard shoulder straps had no device. The headgear was the *Tschapska*, or lance cap, with relevant state badge, cockades and field sign.

Jäger zu Pferde: Mounted Rifles

	Regimental Piping	**Buttons**	**Corps**
Regiment Königs Jäger zu Pferde Nr 1	White	Nickel	V
Jäger Regiment zu Pferde Nr 2	Red	Nickel	XI
Jäger Regiment zu Pferde Nr 3	Yellow	Nickel	XV
Jäger Regiment zu Pferde Nr 4	Light Blue	Nickel	XVII
Jäger Regiment zu Pferde Nr 5	Black	Nickel	XIV
Jäger Regiment zu Pferde Nr 6	Dark Blue	Nickel	XI
Jäger Regiment zu Pferde Nr 7	Rose	Nickel	VIII
Jäger Regiment zu Pferde Nr 8	White	Tombak	VIII
Jäger Regiment zu Pferde Nr 9	Red	Tombak	I
Jäger Regiment zu Pferde Nr 10	Yellow	Tombak	I
Jäger Regiment zu Pferde Nr 11	Light Blue	Tombak	VI
Jäger Regiment zu Pferde Nr 12	Black	Tombak	XVI
Jäger Regiment zu Pferde Nr 13	Dark Blue	Tombak	XVI

Other distinctions: the *Jäger zu Pferde* wore a grey-green *Waffenrock*, with standing collar and Swedish cuffs and regimentally coloured pipings. At the outbreak of war regiments 1–7, and the officers of the remaining regiments were wearing a black metal helmet: other ranks of regiments 8–13 were still wearing dragoon style *Pickelhauben*. Regiment Nr 1 wore a cypher on the shoulder strap whilst the others wore numerals.

ARTILLERY

Field Artillery, or *Feldartillerie*

1. *Garde-Feldartillerie-Regiment.*
2. *Garde-Feldartillerie-Regiment.*
3. *Garde-Feldartillerie-Regiment.*
4. *Garde-Feldartillerie-Regiment.*

Feldartillerie-Regiment Prinz August von Preußen(1. Litthauisches) Nr 1

1. *Pommersches Feldartillerie-Regiment Nr 2*

Feldartillerie-Regiment General Feldzeugmeister (1. Brandenburgisches) Nr 3

Feldartillerie-Regiment Prinz-Regent Luitpold von Bayern (Magdeburgisches) Nr 4

Feldartillerie-Regiment von Podbielski (1. Niederschlesisches) Nr 5

Feldartillerie-Regiment von Peucker (1. Schlesisches) Nr 6

1. *Westfälisches Feldartillerie-Regiment Nr 7*

Feldartillerie-Regiment von Holtzendorff (1.Rheinisches) Nr 8

Feldartillerie-Regiment General-Feldmarschall Graf Waldersee (Schleswigsches) Nr 9

1. *Kurhessisches Feldartillerie-Regiment Nr 11*
1. *Sächsisches Feldartillerie-Regiment Nr 12*

Feldartillerie-Regiment König Karl (1. Württembergisches) Nr 13

Feldartillerie-Regiment Großzog (1. Badisches) Nr 14

1. *Ober-Elsässisches Feldartillerie-Regiment Nr 15*
1. *Ostpreußisches Feldartillerie-Regiment Nr 16*
2. *Pommersches Feldartillerie-Regiment Nr 17*

Feldartillerie-Regiment General-Feldzeugmeister (2. Brandenburgisches) Nr 18

1. *Thüringisches Feldartillerie-Regiment Nr 19*
1. *Posensches Feldartillerie-Regiment Nr 20*

Feldartillerie-Regiment von Clausewitz (1. Oberschlesisches) Nr 21

2. *Westfälisches Feldartillerie-Regiment Nr 22*
2. *Rheinisches Feldartillerie-Regiment Nr 23*

Holsteinsches Feldartillerie-Regiment Nr 24

Großherzoglich Hessisches Feldartillerie-Regiment Nr 25

2. *Hannoversches Feldartillerie-Regiment Nr 26*
1. *Nassauisches Feldartillerie-Regiment Nr 27*
2. *Sächsisches Feldartillerie-Regiment Nr 28*
2. *Württembergisches Feldartillerie-Regiment Prinz-Luitpold von Bayern Nr 29*
2. *Badisches Feldartillerie-Regiment Nr 30*
1. *Unter-Elsässisches Feldartillerie Regiment Nr 31*
3. *Sächsisches Feldartillerie Regiment Nr 32*
1. *Lothringisches Feldartillerie-Regiment Nr 33*
2. *Lothringisches Feldartillerie-Regiment Nr 34*
1. *Westpreußisches Feldartillerie-Regiment Nr 35*
2. *Westpreußisches Feldartillerie-Regiment Nr 36*

2. *Litthauisches Feldartillerie-Regiment Nr 37*
Vorpommersches Feldartillerie-Regiment Nr 38
Kürmarkisches Feldartillerie-Regiment Nr 39
Altmärkisches Feldartillerie-Regiment Nr 40
2. *Niederschlesisches Feldartillerie-Regiment Nr 41*
2. *Schlesisches Feldartillerie-Regiment Nr 42*
Clevesches Feldartillerie-Regiment Nr 43
Triersches Feldartillerie-Regiment Nr 44
Lauenburgisches Feldartillerie-Regiment Nr 45
Niedersächsisches Feldartillerie-Regiment Nr 46
2. *Kurhessisches Feldartillerie-Regiment Nr 47*
4. *Sächsisches Feldartillerie-Regiment Nr 48*
3. *Württembergisches Feldartillerie-Regiment Nr 49*
3. *Badisches Feldartillerie-Regiment Nr 50*
2. *Ober-Elsässisches Feldartillerie-Regiment Nr 51*
3. *Ostpreußisches Feldartillerie-Regiment Nr 52*
Hinterpommersches Feldartillerie-Regiment Nr 53
Neumärkisches Feldartillerie-Regiment Nr 54
2. *Thüringisches Feldartillerie-Regiment Nr 55*
Posensches Feldartillerie-Regiment Nr 56
Oberschlesisches Feldartillerie-Regiment Nr 57
Mindensches Feldartillerie-Regiment Nr 58
Bergisches Feldartillerie-Regiment Nr 59
Großherzoglich Mecklenburgisches Feldartillerie-Regiment Nr 60
2. *Großherzoglich Hessisches Feldartillerie-Regiment 61*
Ostfriesisches Feldartillerie-Regiment Nr 62
2. *Nassauisches Feldartillerie-Regiment Nr 63*
5. *Sächsisches Feldartillerie-Regiment Nr 64*
4. *Württembergisches Feldartillerie-Regiment Nr 65*
4. *Badisches Feldartillerie-Regiment Nr 66*
2. *Unter-Elsässisches Feldartillerie-Regiment Nr 67*
6. *Sächsisches Feldartillerie-Regiment Nr 68*
3. *Lothringisches Feldartillerie-Regiment Nr 69*
4. *Lothringisches Feldartillerie-Regiment Nr 70*
Feldartillerie-Regiment 'Groß-Komtur' Nr 71
Feldartillerie-Regiment 'Hochmeister' Nr 72
1. *Masurisches Feldartillerie-Regiment Nr 73*
Torgauer Feldartillerie-Regiment Nr 74
Mansfelder Feldartillerie-Regiment Nr 75
5. *Badisches Feldartillerie-Regiment Nr 76*
7. *Sächsisches Feldartillerie-Regiment Nr 77*
8. *Sächsisches Feldartillerie-Regiment Nr 78*
3. *Ostpreußisches Feldartillerie-Regiment Nr 79*
3. *Ober-Elsässisches Feldartillerie-Regiment Nr 80*
Thorner Feldartillerie-Regiment Nr 81
2. *Masurisches Feldartillerie-Regiment Nr 82*
3. *Rheinisches Feldartillerie-Regiment Nr 83*
Straßburger Feldartillerie-Regiment Nr 84

Bavarian Field Artillery

1. *Feldartillerie-Regiment Prinz-Regent Luitpold*

2. *Feldartillerie-Regiment Horn*
3. *Feldartillerie-Regiment Prinz Leopold*
4. *Feldartillerie-Regiment König*
5. *Feldartillerie-Regiment König Alfons XIII von Spanien*
6. *Feldartillerie-Regiment Prinz Ferdinand von Bourbon, Herzog von Calabrien*
7. *Feldartillerie-Regiment Prinz Regent Luitpold*
8. *Feldartillerie-Regiment*
9. *Feldartillerie-Regiment*
10. *Feldartillerie-Regiment*
11. *Feldartillerie-Regiment*
12. *Feldartillerie-Regiment*

Distinctions: Field Artillery regiments wore the field grey *Waffenrock* with Swedish cuffs; the collar and cuffs were piped black, the front edge and rear skirts of the jacket were piped scarlet. Shoulder straps were piped according to Corps district being scarlet for the Bavarians and III, IV, XI, XIII, XIV, XV, XIX districts and regiments Nr 25 and 61; white for I, II, IX, X and XII districts; yellow for V, VI, XVI, and XVII districts, plus the *Garde Nr 3*: blue for districts VII, VIII, XVIII and XX; and green for XXI Army Corps district. Shoulder strap numerals and devices were in red, the *Garde* using various forms of grenade without a numeral. In other regiments a grenade was worn above the number or below the cypher. Saxon shoulder straps were distinguished by their square cut tops. Trousers were piped scarlet. The dress headgear was the leather *Kügelhelm*, or 'ball helmet', for all except Bavarian units which wore the spiked *Pickelhaube*. State and *Reichs* cockades and the appropriate state helmet plates were worn.

Foot or *Fußartillerie*

Garde-Fußartillerie-Regiment
Fußartillerie-Regiment von Linger (Ostpreußisches) Nr 1
Fußartillerie-Regiment von Hindersin (1 Pommersches) Nr 2
Fußartillerie-Regiment General-Feldzeugmeister (Brandenburgisches) Nr 3
Fußartillerie-Regiment Encke (Magdeburgisches) Nr 4
Niederschleisisches Fußartillerie-Regiment Nr 5
Fußartillerie-Regiment von Dieskau (Schlesisches) Nr 6
Westfälisches Fußartillerie-Regiment Nr 7
Rheinisches Fußartillerie-Regiment Nr 8
Schleswig-Holsteinisches Fußartillerie-Regiment Nr 9
Niedersächsisches Fußartillerie-Regiment Nr 10
Westpreußisches Fußartillerie-Regiment Nr 11
1. Sächsisches Fußartillerie-Regiment Nr 12
Hohenzollernsches Fußartillerie-Regiment Nr 13
Badisches Feldartillerie-Regiment Nr 14
2. Pommersches Fußartillerie-Regiment Nr 15

Lothringisches Fußartillerie-Regiment Nr 16
2. Westpreußisches Fußartillerie-Regiment Nr 17
Thüringisches Fußartillerie-Regiment Nr 18
2. Sächsisches Fußartillerie-Regiment Nr 19
Lauenburgisches Fußartillerie-Regiment Nr 20

Bavarian Foot Artillery

1. *Fußartillerie-Regiment von Bothmer*
2. *Fußartillerie-Regiment*
3. *Fußartillerie-Regiment*

Distinctions: the basic Foot Artillery uniform of 1914 was similar to that of the field artillery, except that the cuffs were of the Brandenburg type. Foot artillery shoulder straps were piped white, with the exception of Saxon units whose piping was red.

PIONEERS AND OTHER TECHNICAL TROOPS

The field grey *Waffenrock* with stand and fall collar and Swedish cuffs was worn by pioneers (30 battalions of which existed in 1914) and by other technical troops. The jacket was piped scarlet front and rear, with a black collar piping for the Pioneers, Air Service, Telegraph and communication troops and blue piping for Train units. Shoulder strap pipings were scarlet for the Pioneers; blue for Train units; and light grey for Air Service, Telegraph and communication troops. The shoulder straps of such units were further distinguished by the following devices:

Aeroplane units	Winged Propellor
Airship and balloon units	Letter 'L'
Railway Troops	Letter 'E'
Telegraph and telephone units	Letter 'T'
Mechanical Transport units	Letter 'K'
Experimental Pioneer companies	Letter 'V'
Saxon Pioneers	Crossed pick and shovel

Headgear for flying, signal, and airship units was the *Tschako*, whilst pioneers and railway units wore the *Pickelhaube*.

The New Uniform of 1915

After a costly year of war which had seen a massive assault in the west grind to a halt on the Marne, and titanic struggles in the east in which victory appeared to have been wrested from the jaws of defeat at Tannenberg it was apparent that the whole question of service dress was in drastic need of overhaul. What was required was a more practical and less complex uniform. So it was that a new field service dress was announced by the Kaiser through the medium of an *Allerhöchste Kabinetts - Ordre*, number 735, dated 21 September 1915. 'New', as it turned out, was only a relative word, since some of the features of the 1915 uniform were drawn straight from the existing undress *Litewka*, others appeared to come from simplifications already put into practice and certain of the inspirations may have come from Prussian military outfits in use as early as the Napoleonic period.

The basic garment of the 1915 uniform was the *Bluse*, the literal English translation being 'blouse', as was later applied to battledress 'blouses'. This very loose fitting jacket was in field grey (or grey-green for *Jäger*, *Schützen* and *Jäger zu Pferde*), and had a stand and fall collar. This collar was faced with *Abzeichen Tuch*, or 'badge cloth' of a darker and greener colour than the main body of the jacket. Small collar *Litzen* were worn where appropriate, but no pipings on the body of the jacket. The cuffs were simple deep turn backs without any *Litzen*, and the coat had a fly fastening front with concealed buttons. The shoulder straps and skirt pockets were furnished with small dull buttons. Provision 11 of the 21 September order specified that musicians' swallows nests, gorgets, and shooting badges were not to be worn with the *Bluse*.

Though the Guards retained shoulder strap pipings indicating regimental seniority, the Army Corps distinctions used by the rest of the army were abandoned, at least in part because the demands of security and the reorganisations of Corps and Armies were making them increasingly irrelevant. In their stead a new system of arm of service colours was introduced using the following colours:

'1915' Shoulder Strap

Colour	Arm of Service
White (piping only)	Infantry except Guards
Light Green (piping only)	*Jäger* and *Schützen*
Black (piping only)	*Garde Schützen*
Black strap, Scarlet piping	Pioneers
Scarlet or Yellow strap without piping	Field and Foot Artillery
Dark blue, cornflower blue piping	Medical orderlies
Light Grey without piping	Railway, airship, and flying units
White strap with regimental piping	*Kürassier* (cavalry)
Cornflower blue with regimental piping	Dragoons (cavalry)
Scarlet with regimental piping	*Ulanen* (cavalry)

Exceptions to the above were infantry regiments 168 with red piping; 118 with yellow; 117 and 145 with blue and 114 with green piping.

Regimental numbers or devices were kept on the shoulder straps, usually in red, but sometimes in yellow or white for cavalry. The horse and field artillery used yellow numerals and devices on their scarlet straps, whilst the foot artillery wore the reverse, scarlet distinctions on yellow straps. *Landsturm* units maintained the same plain coloured shoulder straps that they had worn in 1914. These were blue for infantry; black for pioneers; scarlet for field artillery; and yellow for field artillery. *Landsturm* cavalry wore the uniform of their parent units being distinguished only by the use of the *Landwehr* cross insignia. Officers also wore the *Bluse* with appropriate distinctions and there was a general officers' version. This had concealed buttons at the front and a dull reduced size version of the relevant embroidery on field grey collar patches. It was piped red around the outer edge of the collar and the cuff turn back.

Though it was intended that the *Bluse* replace all types of service jacket in the field it is notable that the 1915 type uniform never succeeded in entirely displacing the old *Waffenrock*, nor the corresponding cavalry garments. Until 1918 a mixture of new and old uniforms continued to be seen, along with various simplified versions of the old *Waffenrock*. Severe shortages of cloth meant that the quality of garments declined, and eventually many were made from shoddy or other recycled fabrics.

The difficulty in obtaining new textiles is illustrated by the fact that it was ordered that flax be planted in Berlin; that substitute fibres were sought from wood byproducts and wild plants; and that on the home front clothing prices inflated by an average of approximately 1000% during the course of the war. Special care was taken to see that those uniforms already in use stayed clean and serviceable as long as possible, as is testified by the survival of *Kleiderkarten*, which were cards filled in stating what was issued to each recruit, and by the existence of official 'washing

An NCO and private relaxing in a garden, June 1918. The NCO wears a neatly tailored fatigue jacket the other man the *Bluse*. Note the death's head on the peaked cap, worn by *Leib* Hussar and Brunswick units. SB.

tariffs'. These tariffs were formulated for use in occupied zones, and specified the prices to be charged by civilians for soldiers' laundry, thus avoiding profiteering. Portable fumigation stations for the cleaning of both soldiers and their equipment were also deployed, which laughingly became known as *Lauseoleums*. Not surprisingly damaged uniforms were repaired and recycled. The result was many jackets that started life as text book 1910 type *Waffenrock*, and finished their service lives with simplified turn back cuffs, replacement collars, or features more usually associated with the *Bluse*.

It was also true that though the 1915 regulations included a simplified field grey greatcoat with dull metal buttons and no coloured collar patches, old type greatcoats continued to be widely used. Other paragraphs of the new uniform order were aimed at the simplicity and practicality of equipment and accessories. Paragraph 17 stated that all leather work, including pistol and binocular cases, was to be dyed black. Paragraph 18 allowed the use of black ankle

boots or *Schnürschuhe* with puttees to all arms, where previously they had been limited to *Jägers* and other specialists. *Pickelhaube* spikes and *Feldzeichen* on other headgear were no longer to be worn at the front. Despite some anomalies the hitherto individualistic unit uniforms which had existed in 1914 now tended to merge into one mass. As Ernst Jünger observed in *Storm of Steel*, soldiers became the new 'workers of war', wearing grey uniforms, grey steel helmets and trudging through grey mud.

Remarkably the 21 September uniform order only applied in Prussia and smaller states whose forces were already fully integrated. Thus it was that a separate order, state number 761, was issued for Württemberg on 10 October, that for Saxony, number 265, appeared on 9 November, and the Bavarian equivalent, issued in the name of the King of Bavaria, did not appear until as late as 1 April 1916. The various texts of these documents were reprinted in *Deutschlands Armee in Feldgrau Kriegs und Friedens – Uniform*, published in Berlin in 1916. Although the main points were similar these decrees enshrined a number of minor state variations. Perhaps most significantly the Bavarian order stated that the *Bayerische Hoheits-Borte*, or chequered lace, was to be worn on the collar of all garments. Officers' *Hoheits-Borte* was silver and blue, other ranks grey and blue.

Similarly, despite the fact that it is known that some Bavarian troops wore other types of trousers, field grey leg wear was specified. Though plain blank rank buttons were often worn on the collar of the Prussian *Bluse*, state arms variants were retained for the Saxons, Hessians, Mecklenburgers and Württembergers. The Bavarians maintained their traditional lion design.

1915 Dress Uniform

The changes of 1915 also saw the formal abandonment of the coloured pre-war dress uniforms of all but the Guard heavy cavalry and certain of the Hussars. In their stead was substituted a smarter version of the field grey for formal occasions, with a *Jäger* and *Schützen* equivalent of grey-green. The war would see few instances of the use of these new uniforms, but it is clear that they were produced on at least a limited scale prior to the cessation of hostilities, were worn by some officers and more widely by

Freikorps personnel in the upheavals which followed the Armistice.

In the new dress uniform, which was optimistically dubbed a 'peace-time' uniform, the style of the jacket approximated to that of the existing *Waffenrock*, and was deep skirted and closed by eight visible buttons down the front. It was piped, and had cuffs of solid colour according to arm of service, in the style of those on the old dress uniforms. The collar of the jacket was of a standing variety, and was similarly of the arm of service colour; the shoulder straps followed the new 1915 system. So it was, for example, that the dress jacket for the field artillery was field grey with Swedish cuffs. It was piped scarlet down the front, on the rear skirts and around the cuffs and collar. The standing collar and the main part of the cuffs were black. The shoulder straps were scarlet with yellow numerals or devices. The shoulder strap numerals of the medical troops were likewise yellow, though those of other troops were in the traditional red. The remaining details of the field grey 1915 dress uniform jackets can be briefly summarised:

Troop type	Collar and Cuffs	Cuff flaps	Piping	Shoulder Strap
Infantry	Red	Red	Red	Grey (Guard white)
Jäger and *Schützen*	Green	-	Green	Green
Garde Schützen	Black	Grey-Green	Green	Green
Pioneers	Black	-	Red	Black
Technical troops	Black	-	Red	Grey
Foot Artillery	Black	Field Grey	Scarlet	Yellow
Train	Blue	-	Blue	Blue
Medical troops	Dark Blue	Field Grey	Dark Blue	Dark Blue
Jäger zu Pferde	Green	-	Regimental	Green
Dragoons	Regimental	-	Regimental	Cornflower Blue

Rank Distinctions

Rank insignia were worn on both the old and new style field uniform, the major categories of distinction being:

General Feldmarschall (field marshal): *Waffenrock* with breast pockets, and scarlet collar patches on which appeared gold embroidery. Shoulder straps of twisted gold and silver cord with crossed batons.
General Oberst: as above but shoulder straps with three stars.
General: as above but shoulder straps with two stars.
Generalleutnant (lieutenant general): as above but shoulder straps with one star.
Generalmajor (major general): as above but unadorned shoulder straps.

Oberst (colonel): shoulder straps of twisted silver cord with two stars.
Oberstleutnant (lieutenant colonel): as above but one star.
Major: as above but unadorned shoulder strap.
Hauptmann or Rittmeister (captain of infantry and cavalry respectively): narrow silver lace shoulder strap with two stars.
Oberleutnant (lieutenant): as above with one star.
Leutnant (second lieutenant): as above but shoulder strap unadorned.
Feldwebel Leutnant: officer quality uniform with silver braid around collar and large collar buttons.
Feldwebel: single braid on collar, double braid on cuffs, large button on either side of collar. Officer's belt, sword and knot.
Vizefeldwebel: single braid around collar and cuffs and a

large button on either side of the collar, officer's sword and knot .

Sergeant: single braid around collar and cuff and a large button on either side of the collar.

Fähnrich: single braid around collar and cuff, officer's sword and knot.

Unteroffizier: single braid around the collar, and a row of braid around the cuff.

Gefreiter: a small button on either side of the collar.

After 1917, collar braid was usually limited to a section four centimetres in length on each wing of the collar.

Fähnrich and Feldwebel-Leutnant were officer training grades.

Other Badges

Despite the intention of creating a new combat uniform of uncluttered simplicity, a variety of proficiency and special purpose badges were worn with both the 1910 uniform and 1915 *Bluse*. These were in two major categories: cloth insignia which appeared on either the sleeve or upper arm, and metal badges, usually with pin backs, which were worn on the breast. The most important of these were:

Arm badge	Meaning
'Lightning' patch on left sleeve	*Starkstromabteilung* (electrical detachment)
Staff and snake, yellow, right sleeve	Medical personnel
Machine gun, upper left arm	Machine-gun marksman
Numeral and 'MW' upper left arm	*Minenwerfer* unit (later 'MW' and number in red on black shoulder strap)
Death's head on sleeve	Flamethrower troops: believed to have been authorised July 1916
Roughly shaped stick grenade upper arm	Close assault troops (not consistently used c.1916–1918)
Horse shoe on sleeve	Farrier

Breast badge	Meaning
Aircraft within crowned wreath	Pilot
Chequered square in crowned wreath	Air observer
Steel helmet and swords in wreath (black)	Wounded once or twice
Steel helmet and swords in wreath (silver)	Wounded three or four times
Steel helmet and swords in wreath (gold)	Five, or disabling wounds

The wound awards or *Verwundeten-Abzeichen*, were worn on the left side of the jacket, and were often certificated. They were first introduced by order of the Kaiser in March 1918, and also applied retrospectively to injuries sustained in action since the start of the war. There were minor variations in the style of the badges and these continued to be manufactured commercially after the Armistice.

Identity Discs *Erkennungsmarken*

Soldiers of all ranks were supposed to wear a metal identity tag around the neck. These proved useful to allied intelligence since they gave the wearer's unit, but they were not an infallible source of information as men were often transferred from depots, or from unit to unit without this being recorded on the tag. There were several different patterns of identity disc made during the course of the war but in general the earlier types, up to 1915, were in one solid piece, whilst those manufactured from 1916 onward were made with a perforation. These later tags could be snapped in two, leaving one half with the casualty whilst the other part was taken for records purposes.

Helmets, Field Caps and Armour

Pickelhaube

The *Pickelhaube* or spiked helmet was arguably the most distinctive and most varied item worn by the Imperial German army. The original *Pickelhaube*, which has been described as the product of 'artistic whim' rather than military necessity, was introduced for wear by the majority of Prussia's infantry regiments in 1842 as part of King Friedrich Wilhelm IV's reorganisation and re-equipment of the army. The first model was dramatic, being a dome of thick leather 35cm in height, and having massive front and rear peaks. Its practicality was limited by the fact that if worn squarely on the head it restricted vision, and was thus often to be seen slightly tipped back on the cranium. Its great height gave a tendency to instability when the wearer was running or fighting. The new headgear first saw active service against a revolt in Baden in 1849, at which time it was realised that the shiny metal fittings could be a liability in terms of giving away the position of troops trying to hide themselves, and in an order which presaged the events of 1914 and 1915, the application of black lacquer to the fittings was instructed.

The usefulness of the *Pickelhaube* was slightly improved in the middle 1850s by a reduction in size, and it was further modified in the light of experience gained in the Seven Weeks' War of 1866, and the Franco–Prussian War of 1870. Changes brought in during 1887 were aimed at improving the chin strap and slightly simplifying the manufacture of other ranks *Pickelhauben*, the large scale production of which was proving very expensive. The general adoption of a cloth cover or *Uberzuge* came in 1892. Many photographs taken prior to the war show covers, often with coloured bands around them to aid the identification of 'friendly' and 'enemy' troops during exercises.

Further alterations to helmet plate fittings and other details were made in 1895, with the result that

the *Pickelhauben* worn at the outbreak of the Great War are sometimes referred to as the '1895' model or pattern. By this time the private purchase spiked helmet was becoming such a fashion statement for the young German officer that there was a good deal of rivalry aimed at seeing who could procure the hat with the tallest spike. The result was a War Ministry order of May 1899 which regulated the height of the officers' spike to 9.5cm.

The parts of the other ranks *Pickelhaube* in 1914 were numerous, and each was referred to by a specific German nomenclature. Starting at the top the *Spitze* or spike itself was said to be an allusion to the classical spear point. This was mounted on a *Spitzenhals* or spike neck, perforated with ventilation holes or *Luftlocher*. The spike assembly was fitted to the helmet shell by means of a circular base, fixed by locating studs or *Kopfspline*. Artillery units, excepting those of Bavaria, wore a ball fitting in place of the spike. The fittings were usually of brass.

On formal occasions the *Pickelhaube* of elite regiments could be worn with a parade plume, or *Haarbusch*, made of horse hair or similar material. For this purpose the spike would be removed and replaced with a *Haarbuschtrichter*, a parade plume holder consisting of a tall hollow metal stem. From this the parade plume fell down to a point level with the bottom edge of the rear neck guard for officers, though it was worn somewhat shorter by other ranks. The usual colours for the *Haarbusch* were black for the grenadiers; white for Guards and staff officers; red for musicians. Interestingly a white *Haarbusch* cost more than the black: Wilhelm Voigt, outfitters of Magdeburg, were recorded as charging 4.5 Marks for the former and just 2.5 Marks for the latter.

The helmet body itself, or *Helmkopf*, was of hard-boiled or 'jacked' leather, generally stitched up the back and coated with shellac to produce a high gloss black finish. By 1914 the thickness of the leather used was not much more than 1mm. A metal spine or

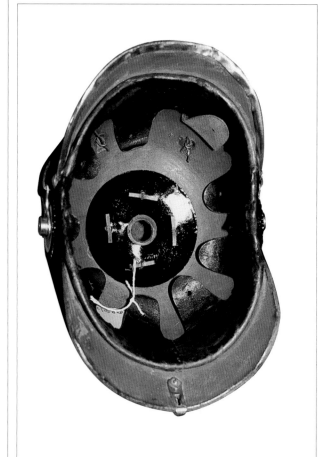

Side view of a typical Prussian infantryman's *Pickelhaube*, with polished leather skull, brass fittings and the state black, white, black cockade.

Interior view of an other ranks leather *Pickelhaube* showing the arrangement of the liner and fittings.

Helmrucken was fitted up the back of the helmet body improving both appearance and rigidity, and ran down over the *Halswache* or neck guard. The metal spine usually incorporated a small ventilation shutter or *Luftungsvorrichtung*. The front peak, described in German as the *Vorderschirm* was fitted with a mount or reinforcement known as the *Vorderschirmschiene*. A comfortable fit for the headgear was ensured internally by a brow band, and a leather liner which was held together by a lace.

The model 1891 chin strap, or *Kinnriemen*, was adjusted by means of buckles, and was held onto the helmet by side posts over and just forward of the wearer's ears. These posts were the model 1891 *Knopf*; and between the helmet body and the chin strap, also fitted over the knob, was the small distinguishing metal rosette known as the *Kokarde* or cockade.

Above.

A *Baden* other ranks infantry *Ersatz Pickelhaube*. In this instance the body of the helmet is made of pressed felt.
Queen's Lancashire Regiment.

Right.

A French cartoonist's view of the way the British would be expected to use the 'spiked helmet'. SB.

Particularly useful in terms of unit identification was the helmet plate or *Wappen* literally 'arms', which was applied to the skull of the helmet by means of small rings, which passed through the skull and were held in place on the inside by small pieces of leather which passed through the rings. Some helmet plates were in two parts with a shield, star, or other device forming a centre-piece.

Officers' *Pickelhauben* varied in many small details of decoration and quality. For example the spike base of an officer's *Pickelhaube* was usually cruciform in shape rather than circular. Most officer grade helmets were also fitted with a *Perlring*, literally a 'ring of pearls' feature, at the base of the spike. This decorative metal ring was not used on other ranks headgear after about 1890, but was available as a private purchase option for non-commissioned officers

A Mecklenburg-Schwerin artillery officer's *Kügelhelm*; note the metal chin scales and *Perlring* around the spike typical of officer quality headgear.

A Prussian Guards officer's *Pickelhaube* complete with white parade plume or Haarbusch.

and One Year volunteers. Similarly commissioned officers, and some non-commissioned officers, were entitled to use chin scales rather than a plain leather chin strap. Officers' *Pickelhauben* were also distinguished by the quality of their linings which were of linen or silk, and the underside of the officers' helmet peak was often coloured in green and the neck guard in red. General officers, certain staff officers, and Bavarian officers had a fluted rather than a plain spike. Officers *Pickelhauben* were purchased privately, and on the eve of war a very basic model without any extras cost about 21 Marks. Parade plumes and materials of superior quality could easily double this price.

As has been intimated, the *Pickelhaube* was not merely an emblem of German identity but a repository of local state symbolism. The main features which allow one to 'read' a *Pickelhaube* are the *Wappen* and the *Kokarden*, which varied from state to state and from unit to unit. The cockade system as it applied in 1914 meant that the 'Reichs' or 'Empire' *Kokarde* was mounted on the right side of the *Pickelhaube*, the

colours of this rosette, from the centre to the outside ring being red, white and black. The left cockade, or state cockade, was as follows:

State	Left Cockade (working from centre outward)
Anhalt	Green
Baden	Gold / Red / Gold
Bavaria	White / Blue / White
Brunswick	Dark Blue / Yellow / Dark Blue
Hanseatic states	Red / White /Red (or red cross on white)
Hesse-Darmstadt	White / Red / White / Red / White
Lippe-Detmold	Red / Yellow
Mecklenburg	Red/ Yellow / Dark Blue
Oldenburg	Dark Blue / Red / Dark Blue
Prussia	Black / White / Black
Reuss	Black / Red / Gold
Saxe-Weimar	Black / Yellow / Green
Saxony	White / Green / White
Thuringia	Green / White / Green
Schwarzburg-	

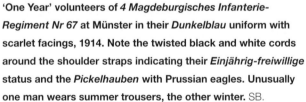

'One Year' volunteers of *4 Magdeburgisches Infanterie-Regiment Nr 67* at Münster in their *Dunkelblau* uniform with scarlet facings, 1914. Note the twisted black and white cords around the shoulder straps indicating their *Einjährig-freiwillige* status and the *Pickelhauben* with Prussian eagles. Unusually one man wears summer trousers, the other winter. SB.

The young Joachim Ernst, Duke of Anhalt, wearing a particularly splendid Anhalt officer's *Pickelhaube*. It has the Anhalt helmet plate with the arms of the Duchy on the breast of a Prussian eagle and the officer's *Perlring* around the base of the spike. The chin strap is of metal scales and the Anhalt cockade was green. SB.

Sonderhausen	White / Dark Blue / White
Waldeck	Black / Red / Yellow
Württemburg	Black / Red / Black

The position concerning the *Wappen* or helmet plate was if anything more complex, a large number of variations being recorded, with distinctions, particularly in terms of mottoes, and differences in quality between those of officers and other ranks. The major types were as follows:

State / Units	Wappen
Anhalt	Prussian eagle with arms of Anhalt superimposed
Baden	Griffin clutching sword and shield
Baden *Leib Grenadier*	As above but with star and cross superimposed
Bavaria	Bavarian arms with lion supporters and crown
Brunswick	Prussian eagle, skull superimposed; or horse on cross, on starburst
Hanseatic states	Prussian eagle clutching orb and sceptre
Hesse	Rampant lion clutching sword, surrounded by leaves
Mecklenburg	Mecklenburg arms and crown on 12-pointed starburst
Oldenburg	Prussian eagle with arms of Oldenburg superimposed
Prussia	Prussian eagle, clutching orb and sceptre
Prussian Line Infantry	As above 'FR' cypher on eagle
Prussian Dragoons	Prussian eagle clutching sword and sceptre

A fine selection of *Mützen*. Top row left to right: Prussian artillery officer's dress cap with black velvet band and scarlet pipings; officer's cap *Leib-Husaren* Regiment Nr 2, with black band, white piping and *Totenkopf* or death's head between the cockades; Prussian officer's soft field cap artillery, engineers or air service with black band and scarlet piping; Mecklenburg *Jäger* NCOs peaked cap in grey-green material, with green band and piping and Mecklenburg lower cockade.

Centre row, left to right: Bavarian medical officer's cap with blue band, red piping and Bavarian lower cockade; officer's cap Prussian *Garde Ulanen* Regiment Nr 3 with yellow band and piping; Prussian *Jäger* NCOs cap in grey-green material with green band and piping; Prussian infantry NCOs cap with scarlet band and piping.

Bottom row, left to right: Prussian other ranks cap with scarlet piping and grey camouflage strip covering the band; Prussian *Jäger* other ranks cap with green band and piping; other ranks flying service cap with black band and scarlet piping, (similar to that worn by artillery); Baden other rank reservist's cap with scarlet band and piping, the lower Baden cockade bearing the Reserve cross. Alan Beadle Antique Arms and Militaria.

Prussian Guard Prussian eagle clutching sword and sceptre; Guard Star superimposed

Saxony   Saxon arms and crown on eight-pointed starburst

Württemburg Württemburg arms with stag and lion supporters

Reservists, *Landwehr* and *Landsturm* were further differentiated by the integration of crosses into the *Wappen*. Prussian *Landwehr* usually had a cross superimposed upon the breast of the Prussian eagle, whilst Prussian reservists wore a small cross between the eagle's legs. Saxon reservists had a cross between the arms and the starburst; whilst Baden reservists had a cross in the centre of the Griffin's shoulder. In the case of reservists from Bavaria a slender cross was integrated into the state arms. Württemburg and Mecklenburg used a cross on the centre of their arms to represent reservists.

During the eastern and western front campaigns of 1914 and 1915 the *Pickelhaube* was usually worn with its cover. Officially this was rush green in colour, but examples in field grey and even brown were fairly commonplace. In the case of the standard other ranks cover, it was held in place by five hooks, three to the front and two to the rear of the *Pickelhaube*. This arrangement, though it worked well enough, was inclined to look scruffy, and officers' covers and other

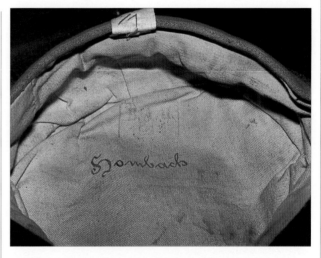

private purchase pieces tended to be made with a pocket arrangement into which the front and rear peaks of the headgear were fitted. Initially, the covers were marked with the regimental number in red felt, except for the Guards whose cover was plain. During August 1914, however, the numbers were changed to green, and very often these were stencilled on in paint; and with time the size of the numerals tended to decrease. Technically, whilst line regiments were to use just their number marked in Arabic numerals, reserve regiments were to prefix the number with the letter 'R'; *Ersatz* reservists with a letter 'E'; *Landwehr* with the letter 'L'; and *Landsturm* with a small cross. In practice, however, *Ersatz* reserves were often sent to fill up the line, and *Landwehr* and *Landsturm* often lacked the latest headgear. Photographic evidence suggests that prefixes other than the 'R' were not commonly seen, and that quite early on many units dispensed with numbers on their *Pickelhauben* altogether. The wearing of plain covers became

mandatory throughout the army at about the end of 1915.

Within days of the start of the war, supplies of *Pickelhauben* fell behind the numbers of recruits coming into the army. Pretty rapidly, corners began to be cut and helmets of obsolete types saw service. In some units there were not enough helmet plates of the right patterns, resulting in mismatches or the issue of Prussian eagles where theoretically other symbols should have been worn. Within a few months there were material shortages and cheaper metals were being treated to make them appear like brass or silver;

leather became scarcer as cheap supplies from South America were cut off. A whole industry developed in the use of *Ersatz* or 'supplementary' materials, and *Pickelhaube* shells began to be made of substances as diverse as tin plate, steel, fibre board, cork, papier mache and felt fabricated from rabbit fur or wool. One manufacturer even proposed the use of thin wood, but

A very young member of the *2. Ersatz Landsturm battalion Arolsen Nr 20*, of XI Army Corps district, pictured at Göttingen in September 1917. The headgear is the distinctive *Landsturm* oil cloth cap, but contrary to regulation the old blue uniform is still worn. SB.

Officer's lance cap, or *Tschapka*, of *Ulanen Regiment Nr 8*.

whether any were so made has not been determined. In many instances these *Ersatz Pickelhauben* were painted black or polished into a thoroughly passable representation of the original, but especially where felt was involved the final colour could be anything from grey, to brown, or even dark green. It is also notable that a *Pickelhaube* for use by expeditionary forces in the tropics had been in existence for some years prior to the war. These were usually of leather but clad in grey felt.

A serious effort was made to standardise *Pickelhaube* production in the latter part of 1915. The most important facet of this drive was the introduction of a new simplified model for other ranks, made of leather, but with steel fittings, a helmet plate painted grey and a somewhat shorter detachable spike. This type has since become known as the 'model' 1915: its advantages were economy in materials, lack of anything shiny to attract enemy fire and ease of cleaning. In September 1915, it was ordered that the

new *Pickelhaube* be worn at the front without the spike, which was now finally acknowledged as more of a liability than an asset on the battlefield. A detachable spike version of the *Pickelhaube* for officers, with brass and zinc fittings, and a cotton or linen liner was also introduced. As might be expected, *Pickelhaube* covers now began to be made without any provision for a spike. The 1915 type *Pickelhaube* continued to be made for about two years by which time the steel helmet had completely replaced it in the trenches, in all but the quietest sectors of the East. It was notable that many officers continued to wear their spiked helmets on formal parades; the Kaiser and senior staff, for example, never seemed to wear the steel helmet.

Field Caps

Apart from the *Pickelhaube* and the steel helmet, the principle types of headgear seen worn with the field grey and grey-green service dress were caps and shakos. The caps were of two main types, peaked and peakless. These were known respectively as the *Dienstmütze*, or service cap, and the *Feldmütze* or field cap, and the main colour of the material from which they were cut was either field grey or grey-green to agree with the rest of the uniform. The visorless *Feldmütze* was frequently worn by other ranks in the trenches, or with the fatigue dress. It was essentially a soft cap, without any stiffening. The *Dienstmütze* which had a black leather peak and chin strap was worn by all ranks behind the lines, but on campaign was usually limited to officers and non-commissioned officers. As part of a 'walking out dress', or for formal situations, it was normally neat and well-shaped with the aid of stiffening around the crown. In the field or at work, less crisp; and sometimes rather shapeless, 'crusher' types without stiffening predominated.

Both the *Dienstmütze* and the *Feldmütze* were differentiated as to state and arm of service. The state affiliation could be determined by means of two cockades worn one above the other on the front of the cap which were essentially miniature versions of the cockades worn on either side of the *Pickelhaube*. The upper one was the *Deutsche* or *Reichs Kokarde*, red, white and black in concentric rings working outward; the lower one the state cockade or *Landeskokarde*, the

various colours of which can be found in the section relating to the *Pickelhaube* above. The arm of service was given by the colour of the cap band and welt as follows:

Arm of Service	Cap band	Welt or piping
Infantry	Scarlet	Scarlet
Jäger	Green	Green
Schützen	Black with green edging	Green
Artillery, engineers, air service	Black with scarlet edging	Scarlet
Train (supply) troops	Light blue	Light blue
Cavalry	Regimental	Regimental

On campaign the *Feldmütze* was usually worn with the coloured cap band covered by a strip of grey cloth to aid concealment. This band was buckled and adjustable at the rear and at the front was frequently provided with a slit through which the lower cockade appeared. In July 1917 an order was issued for the

Other ranks Prussian Jäger shako, dated 1915. Note the black and white field sign and the grey painted metal eagle shako plate.

Interior of the same shako showing the arrangement of the leather liner.

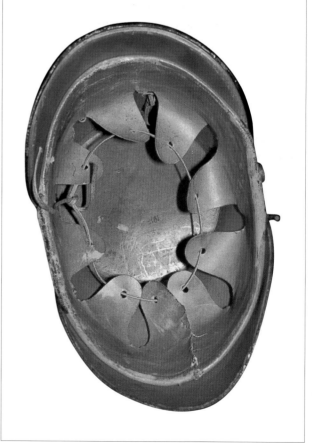

Front and side views of the Model 1916 steel helmet. The field grey example is a small size fitting with two stage side lugs; the camouflaged piece is a large size with the single stage lug.

introduction of an *Einheits–Feldmütze* or universal forage cap, which lacked the coloured band altogether and instead had both band and crown made of field grey, or grey-green, material, and in the last months of the war, soft peaked caps in field grey were issued pretty well irrespective of rank. So it was that by the Armistice that, even within the same unit, a variety of caps might be worn, peaked and peakless, with and without coloured bands.

A soft peaked cap, similar in shape to that worn by the Austrian army, was worn by mountain units and is described in the section on special clothing. Finally one other type of cap quite commonly seen was the special pattern worn by the *Landsturm*. This was peaked, had an oil cloth crown and was not as broad in the top as the ordinary *Dienstmütze*. In photographs it thus appears shiny and rather cylindrical. Instead of two cockades, a brass *Landwehr* style cross was worn over a single national cockade on the band.

Tschakos and Tschapka

The *Tschako* or shakos in use were of several distinct types, but fell into two general categories: those recent types worn by the *Jägers* and *Schützen*; and those obsolete models often used by the *Landsturm* and *Landwehr*. The *Jäger* shako current for most units at the outbreak of war was the Model 1895, a hat of polished black leather which tapered, was shaped to the back of the head and had a small and relatively low crown. It was fitted with front and rear peaks, a black leather chin strap, and had small lacquered ventilation grills on either side. The issue shako was fitted with a tan leather liner, and often stamped internally with the date of manufacture. Beneath the right hand chin strap boss was secured the national cockade of red, white and black, and projecting above the centre of the top rim was an oval cloth field badge. In the case of Prussian units this had a black centre and a white outer: Mecklenburg had an inner field quartered carmine and dark blue over which was a yellow cross, all within a yellow outer; and *Jäger* Battalion Nr 7 showed the colours of Schaumburg-Lippe with a blue centre, red inner, and white outer. Bavarian units had a field badge with an inner field of light blue and a white outer. For parades, black horsehair plumes were worn

PLATE 4.   166

Helmet and Shako Ornaments.

Troops of the Guard.

G. du Corps and
G. Cuirassiers.

Body Gd.
Hussars.

G. Jäger, Train
and Schützen.

Gren. R. 2, 7, 8.
Drag. No. I.
Horse Gren. R. No. 3.
(Silver.)

Old Prussian
Eagle.

gle worn by
Line Regts.

N.C.O.'s Schools.

Drag. Regts.

Hus. Regts. 1
and 2.

Hus. Regt. 7.

Hus. Regt. 17.

Bavaria.

Saxony.

Württemberg.

Baden No. 109
Gren. R.

Baden.

Hesse.

Meckl.-Schwerin.

Meckl.-Strelitz.

Oldenburg.

Saxe Weimar.

Brunswick.

Brunswick.
Inf. Reg. 92, III Battn.

Anhalt.

Saxon Duchies.

Schwarzburg.

Reuss.

by most units except the Bavarians, with red plumes for musicians.

The shako badge for the majority of the *Jäger* battalions was a Prussian eagle bearing the inscription *Mit Gott Fur Koenig und Vaterland* on a scroll. *Jäger* Battalion Nr 10 had a circular scroll in addition with Waterloo, Peninsula and Venta del Pozo battle honours. Guard units wore the Guard star, and Bavarians their state arms and the motto *In Treue Fest*. The Guard badge was in German silver whilst other units had badges in dark bronze or tombak, but from 1915 grey painted fittings began to be used. The 1895 model shako was often worn in the field with grey-green cover, through which the field badge was displayed. Both plain covers and covers with green numerals have been observed.

Saxon *Jäger* units were something of an exception in that they wore a different shako covered in black cloth, with a front peak but no rear peak. Also, the Saxon shako displayed no field badge, having instead two cockades; the national or Reichs cockade on the right; and the Saxon white, green, white cockade on the left. Saxon *Jäger* battalions 12 and 13 wore a star badge in silver on which was a tombak coat of arms and bugle horn; *Schützen* Regiment Nr 108 had a tombak star with silver arms and horn. Saxon *Jägers* wore black parade plumes, rising for the 12th, drooping for the 13th and horizontal for the *Schützen*. The machine-gun detachments or *Maschinengewehr-Abteilungen* also wore a shako at the outbreak of war, their distinctive pattern being of grey-green felt strengthened with tan leather.

The obsolete *Landwehr* and *Landsturm* shakos were generally of the 1860, and 1888 varieties, the now ancient Model 1860 being the taller of the two. These shakos, like those of the *Jäger*, were usually fitted with a field sign. The shako plates were of various patterns, the most common two being the Prussian eagle and the *Landwehr* cross within an oval. Perhaps

surprisingly, photographic evidence suggests that even within the same company shakos with two different badges might be worn. These obsolete shakos were often worn with a cover in the field, with the field badge showing. *Landsturm* units sometimes displayed the cross on the cover.

The lance cap, or *Tschapka*, was a Polish inspired piece of headgear with a polished black leather skull and an upper section shaped not unlike an academic mortar board. There was a front visor and a helmet plate, and the state field sign was worn on the front upper left hand side. Cap lines connected the *Tschapka* with the wearer's uniform, and were intended to prevent the loss of the headgear in action. The

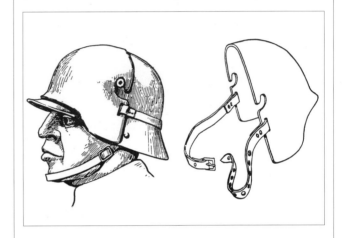

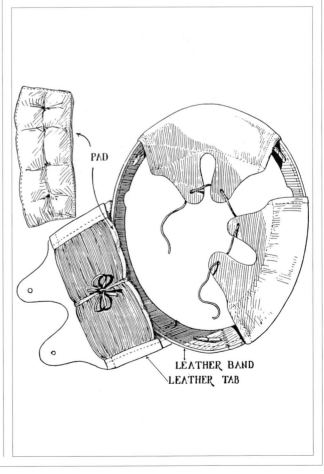

Opposite.

Helmet and shako ornaments as depicted in *Handbook of the German Army*, 1918.

Top right.

Line drawing showing the Model 1916 helmet with its bullet proof brow plate or *Stirnpanzer*. The detachable helmet plate locates over the side lugs and is held in place by means of a buckled strap.

Right.

The liner of the Model 1916 helmet showing how the three pads are held in place behind large tabs on the leather band.

Helmets, Field Caps and Armour 77

Above.

Left side view of the helmet with 1918 type disruptive camouflage.

Left.

Front view of the Model 1916 showing detail of the 1918 'lozenge' type disruptive camouflage pattern, in green, yellow ochre and rust brown, divided by a black line. Queens Lancashire regiment.

Left below.

Liner of the Model 1916, showing the original leather type head band, chin strap and three pad arrangement.

relevant state plates were worn as was the eagle and Guard Star device. For parade wear, the upper part of the lance cap was covered with a distinctively coloured cloth cover or *Rabatte*, and a white drooping plume was worn. On active service the lance cap was worn with a field grey cover.

Steel Helmet

Soon after the outbreak of the Great War many nations discovered that a disproportionate number of head wounds were occurring. In the German instance

Above.

Side view of a large size Model 1918 helmet shell with disruptive 1918 type camouflage. A very dull finish has been achieved by using green and rust brown and sprinkled with sand. SB.

Right.

Late type Model 1916 helmet interior, with sheet steel band and more cheaply-made pads.

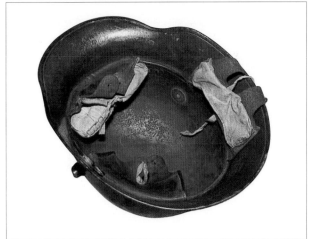

Right below.

Detail of chin strap attachment on the Model 1916, showing the Model 1891 Pickelhaube style pillar over which the metal loop on the end of the strap locates. Notice also the rolled edge of the helmet rim.

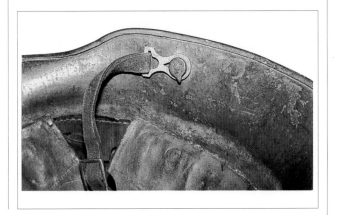

it was observed that heads poked above the level of earthworks were extremely vulnerable and that the existing *Pickelhauben* and cavalry helmets, which were primarily decorative, were ineffectual against shrapnel. By early 1915 the importance of improved head protection was widely realised: in Army Group Gaede on the rocky Vosges front the local Chief of Staff, Colonel Hesse, went so far as to introduce a small number of steel caps with metal nose guards. These were very heavy at 4.5 lb, and are believed not to have

An assault troop officer wearing the Model 1916 *Stahlhelm*, c. 1917. Other interesting details include the Model 1916 steel trench shield with its closable rifle slit; three stick grenades secured to the belt by means of their hooks; and a 'concentrated charge' suitable for attacking tanks and bunkers, consisting of seven grenade heads on a single stick handle. Ted Neville, TRH Pictures.

exceeded 1,500 examples, but they were a valuable experiment and did point the way to better headgear for the army as a whole.

In the summer of 1915 one of those charged with the treating of brain injuries was Professor Dr August Bier, Navy Surgeon General and consultant to XVIII Army Corps. In his search for better care he called in Captain of Landwehr Dr Friedrich Schwerd who, in civilian life, was professor at the Hanover Technical Institute. Their first co-operation involved the attempted use of a powerful electromagnet in the operating theatre, designed to remove small metal splinters which were otherwise inaccessible in the cerebellum. Despite this innovation Schwerd soon became convinced that he had a more significant role in preventative medicine, in other words to protect heads from injury in the first place.

Professor Bier, therefore, wrote to the medical staff

of 2nd Army supporting Schwerd's initiative with medical facts and figures. For example, it appeared remarkable that out of a total of 102 head wounds examined in a period of less than three months, at least three quarters were caused by shell fragments and tiny pieces of metal at that. As he reported it, the largest fragment was no larger than the 'size of a bean', and most were no larger than the average sized cherry pip, many indeed were even smaller. The conclusion appeared obvious: a strong, light, protective helmet would be perfectly adequate to stop a majority of these missiles, and in doing so would not only alleviate much human misery but would husband medical resources for little outlay. Bier's persuasive remarks were duly reported up the chain of command until they eventually fell on the desk of Von Falkenhayn, Chief of the General Staff of the Field army. In his turn he endorsed the idea and asked the Prussian War Ministry to take action.

By the end of August, the clothing section of the Ministry was working not only with Professor Schwerd but with Krupp of Essen, and Juncker and Company of Berlin; ironically enough Juncker themselves had already submitted an idea for a metal hard hat which had not been progressed. A week later Schwerd came up with a list of specifications for the ideal metal helmet. It would be: a universal issue replacing the leather spiked helmet; of a weight not exceeding 1 kg; preferably double skinned; with neck and forehead protection; of nickel or manganese steel; protective against small fragments though emphatically not bullet proof; ventilated via two vent lugs; anti-rust protected and painted. Though the 'double skinned' feature would be done away with, Schwerd had effectively outlined the new *Stahlhelm* project and its end result in a few sentences. Furthermore, prospective manufacturers were then provisionally identified in the shape of the Silesiahütte and Bismarckhütte works (both of Upper Silesia), Wupperman and also the firm of F Pintsch. Juncker were excluded on the grounds that they did not have the technical ability for processing the necessary metal plates. A few days after this the Pintsch company produced their first experimental prototype.

The familiar shape which had already begun to emerge was governed by a demand that the head be protected as much as possible whilst all-round vision should not be impaired. It had been noted at this stage that the lengths of the side and neck skirt were practically limited by the position of the back pack and the necessity of aiming the rifle in various positions. The resultant contour was, as Schwerd himself observed, something like the *Schallernhelm* of the Middle Ages, with its neck protector standing clear of the neck, extending forward to the temples, and up over the brow in a single sweep to form a peak. For good or ill, one of the most distinctive cultural icons and objects of vilification of the 20th century had been born. Nevertheless, there can be little doubt that Dr Schwerd's primary objective had been life-saving: he was never paid anything, but he did win the Iron Cross First Class at the front – and survived the war.

It was explicitly reiterated at this stage that the new steel helmet was not to be proof against direct small-arms fire, for to be so it would have had to weigh at least 6 kg, and thereby be totally unmanageable. As a sop to bullet resistance during the 'momentary tactical conditions' of trench fighting which pertained in 1915, a detachable frontal shield 5 mm thick, and weighing about 1 kg, was allowed for. In the inventor's ideal world each soldier would be provided with such a plate to carry with his equipment, and on the command *Schutzschilde hoch* the men would clap them to their helmets. In practice this was the one impractical element in the system, and relatively few such shields, now commonly known as 'sniper's plates', were actually made. The plate did, however, account for the two prominent visor lugs which would become an enduring and distinctive characteristic of the Great War German helmet.

The chosen outline and desirable ballistic qualities being thus delineated, the search commenced for sufficient quantities of nickel steel and adequate production facilities for the intended massive output. These factors probably caused more problems than the actual design, metal quality being a particularly sensitive matter. Testing soon revealed that if the metal was not of the right toughness and malleability it would split in the presses or fail to mould to the right shape. Tempering also played a significant part, as did minor variations in metallurgical composition, the combinations of which could lead to significant fluctuations in ballistic resistance.

Perhaps the biggest trial was a somewhat bizarre experiment mounted at the Kummersdorf proving ground on 20 November 1915. Here 400 of the first helmets of two different metal thicknesses were set out on the range, together with a selection of *Pickelhauben* and foreign headgears. These were then systematically pounded with field guns and 10.5 cm howitzers. After more than 60 rounds the resultant tangle of pieces was taken away for analysis, together with the collected results of bullet strike tests and more conventional data. It was observed with much interest by both the University of Berlin and army medical staff, that the products of the various production plants behaved in unexpectedly different ways. Those made by Rochling, for example, almost always showed neat entry holes, and seldom any deformation or fragmentation, but were somewhat brittle. Helmets by Lindenberg and by Krefelder and company, by contrast, showed evidence of dangerous splintering and numbers of 'secondary fragments'. Bismarckhütte helmets were the best for, although they bulged and tore when badly hit, there was only minimal fragmentation. Efforts were therefore made to isolate and reproduce the desirable characteristics whilst avoiding the bad, and in the final version the helmets were painted in an egg shell, field grey finish.

Equally systematic and exhaustive methods were applied to the testing of helmet liners, which were very necessary to diminish shock to the wearer's head in the case of a strike. Areas examined included not only the absorption and elasticity of various materials, but their durability and availability in war-time. The system finally selected comprised a leather band, riveted at three points to the helmet outer shell, to which was attached three cushions stuffed with horse hair. One of the cushions was designed to rest over the brow, whilst the other two were at the sides of the head toward the rear: a clever arrangement since, like the legs of a milking stool on an uneven floor, three

The 1916 Model steel trench or sniper shield. The slit and shutter are slightly offset so as to provide maximum cover to a right handed soldier firing a rifle.

points of contact ensured steadiness whatever the exact shape of the cranium. A perfect fit was further helped by the fact that the helmet shell was itself to be made in no less than six different sizes, '60' to '70' in two cm steps, the size of the head to be accommodated being about eight to ten cm smaller in each instance than the actual shell size. 'Fine tuning' could be carried out by the individual soldier increasing or decreasing the wadding in, or behind, the three liner pockets. Interestingly, small helmets could be distinguished from the large at a glance by the fact that the smaller sizes required a two step visor lug, whilst those from size 64 upward had a simple cylindrical pipe only.

The inventors claimed that the three pad lining system was effective in allowing adequate ventilation and blood circulation. Air was similarly able to enter down the centre void of the visor lugs, so that the *Stahlhelm* did not get unduly hot. Indeed, it was soon recognised that wearers could become cold in winter and that in stormy weather wind whistling through the helmet could impair hearing. To obviate these effects

it was officially recommended that a handkerchief could be worn on the head under the helmet, and that the visor lugs could be blocked with paper or soil. The helmet chin strap was removable, made of leather and mounted onto the underside of the shell apron by means of model 1891 fittings. As with the *Pickelhaube* the strap was removed by rotating the ring at the end of the leather around the lug until a cutout lined up with a 'nose' on the pillar and the strap came free.

The first issue of the new steel helmet for troop trials was made in December 1915, the selected guinea pigs being the men of Captain Rohr's 1st Assault Battalion, who rapidly declared the new headgear a success. Within a month, 30,000 helmets had been made at the Eisenhüttenwerk Thale and were on their way to assault units in the Verdun sector. Since it was now January 1916 the helmet soon became known as the 'Model 1916'. In February, the High Command agreed the issue of steel helmets to the field army in general.

Reports from the front soon confirmed the results of the trials. Systematic questioning of the units fighting at Verdun revealed that the helmet was an excellent protection against small fragments. In some instances soldiers were knocked prostrate by the impact of missiles, yet the helmet shells remained unbroken. In certain cases where larger fragments had actually penetrated, the wearers survived, though rendered unconscious, or wounded. The helmet was not found too heavy for prolonged use and perhaps most importantly it was immediately popular with the front line troops themselves. Far from shunning the steel helmet, any men not so equipped were quick to pick up and use any that had been discarded. Though obviously a great success there were some criticisms: the surface was declared too shiny; the 'sniper's plate' was found impracticably heavy; and many men took to wearing soft headgear under the helmet so as not to become cold.

These easily remedied matters aside, there was nothing to prevent full scale production and a general issue. By July 1916, almost 300,000 helmets had been given to the troops. Once the needs of the Verdun and Somme sectors had been answered, supplies were directed to the rest of the Western Front and then to the East. Finally issues were made to the rear echelons. Individual soldiers set about camouflaging their headgear with foliage, sacking covers and even splodges of paint and mud, but in the winter of 1916 official issues were made of white covers, secured by hooks around the edge, for use in snow. In February 1917, the white cover was joined by a grey cover, the best part of a million of which were eventually manufactured. In May of that year, due to leather shortage, the liner band was changed to sheet steel. Late in the war examples of the helmet were encountered using field dressings instead of horse hair pads in the lining, chin straps which were made of woven cloth or paper instead of leather, and other substitute materials.

None of these modifications or additions is generally thought of as a 'model' change, but in 1918 the old style chin strap fittings were deleted and the strap was henceforth attached direct to the liner band. The new helmet then became known as the 'Model 1918', or M18. Externally the M16 and M18 may be distinguished by the number of rivet heads visible on the surface. The M16 has five, whilst the M18 has only three.

Also in 1918 came the so called 'lozenge' pattern disruptive paint camouflage, which was also used on artillery pieces and machine-guns and was usually applied at unit level. As described in a General Staff circular of 7 July 1918, this pattern was to be of three colours separated by 'finger wide' strips of black paint. On the helmet this was to consist of large, equal, sharp-cornered patches of colour which were to be varied with the season and background scenery. From the front, four colour fields were to be visible and dark and light colours were purposely put next to each other so as to maximise the disruptive effect. Whilst still wet the paint was to be sprinkled with fine sand, creating a non-reflective slightly 'crinkled' surface. The colours recommended and supplied for this camouflage pattern in the summer of 1918 were green, yellow ochre and rust brown, and it appears that these hues predominated, in varying proportions, right up until the end of the war. Insignia were not generally worn on the helmet during the Great War, but it is known that the *Garde zu Fuß* Regiment Nr 1 wore the Hohenzollern arms on the left side of their headgear. This small shield was quartered black and white: black top right and bottom left; white top left and bottom right.

The total production of the German steel helmet in the Great War is believed to be about 7.5 million units. Though the 'standard' M16 and M18 models predominated at least three variations were made in small numbers. The first of these has a shallower angle of incidence to the front, and a greater clearance between the forehead and the helmet. It is generally believed that this rarity was an experiment designed with two possible ends in mind: easier to wear with a gas mask, and a more deflective surface for projectiles. The second major variant was that with cut-outs in the rim (which has prompted all manner of weird and wonderful explanations amongst collectors). In fact a few thousand pieces of this headgear were manufactured in the latter part of 1918, the official explanation from the War Ministry being that they improved the wearer's hearing. These helmets also incorporated improvements to the finish and chin strap. They were issued in small numbers for evaluation in August 1918, together with instructions that reports on their performance should be made by that December. If any such reports were made, none have yet been found, and in any case their relevance would have been overtaken by the end of hostilities. The final significant variation was a strange, peakless model made in 1918 ordered by the Ottoman Empire, but apparently only a limited number had been delivered by the time the war ended. The result was the surplus 'Turkish' helmets were reused by the *Freikorps* in 1919.

Though useful and enduringly popular, the steel helmet was not immune to the usual ribaldry that soldiers visit upon their equipment. Amongst other things it was referred to as the 'cooking pot' or the 'chamber pot'. The jokes obviously translated to some degree since in English the German helmet was soon either a 'coal scuttle' or 'jerry', the latter being current slang for a chamber pot. By an interesting piece of etymology all Germans, previously the 'Hun' or 'Bosche' were soon being called 'Jerries'. Consciously or not, a whole people were now being defined by the shape of a single piece of equipment.

Armour

The main type of body armour used by German forces was the set of plates commonly known as the *Infanterie* or *Sappenpanzer* which entered service in late 1916 and by June 1917 had been issued pretty widely especially within Sixth Army. It consisted of four pieces of silicon-nickel steel armour, articulated together by webbing straps, and padded between the plates with felt to keep the parts from jangling together. The top, or breast plate, was the largest and was hooked over the shoulders by means of two curved pieces at the top. From the breast plate hung three plates of decreasing dimensions which covered the abdomen and groin. The armour sets came in two size fittings, the smaller of which weighed about 9 kg, whilst the larger was just under 11kg. It was capable of resisting small grenade and shell fragments, and could stop a rifle bullet if fired from a range of 300 yards or more. According to one account it was possible not only to wear the armour covering the vulnerable areas of the chest and stomach, but to wear it back to front, so that it covered the back when the wearer was prone or standing up against a breastwork.

The armour met with very mixed reactions from the troops. General Ludendorff intended that it should be used primarily by sentries, machine-gunners and trench garrisons, and to these ends issues were generally made a few per company. When so used the armour was reasonably useful and did prevent casualties. On the other hand the *Sappenpanzer* was less than ideal for any form of rapid manoeuvre, as one report suggested: 'It should not be used for operations which entail crossing obstacles by climbing, jumping or crawling, especially as it makes it difficult to carry ammunition. When the enemy attacks, the armour has to be taken off, as it decreases the mobility of the soldier on account of its weight and stiffness.'

In the last months of the war a second version of the trench armour was introduced, differing only in the addition of stowage hooks to the breast plate and provision for a better position for the butt of the rifle against the shoulder. The 20 or so examples of armour examined by the present writer have all been of the first or '1917' type. The total number of sets issued was about 500,000.

Apart from armour worn on the head and body, there was also use made of small trench plates, or manlets, sometimes known as 'snipers loops'. These could be carried short distances, perhaps by an assault party to help create a 'trench block', but were usually set into the sides of trenches or used to create semi-permanent snipers posts. Though small portable shields were in use even before the start of hostilities, the commonest type used during the war was that generally known as the Model 1916. This consisted of a rectangular plate of silicon-nickel steel about 60 cm long which curved forwards slightly at each end, and weighed approximately 13.5 kg. Offset to one side, so as to be of maximum benefit to a right-handed rifleman, was a vertical slot through which the weapon could be aimed. This slot was fitted with a shutter which could be closed from the inside. On the back of the shield was a prop which would allow the plate to be put up on flat ground. The Model 1916 shield would resist machine-gun fire at ranges over 100 yards, but could be penetrated by armour piercing rounds.

Another manlet, which has been popularly christened the 'Model 1916–1917', was of a generally similar configuration but with several significant differences. Perhaps the most obvious was that the opening took the form of a mouse-hole in the bottom edge of the plate and had no shutter. Another difference was that rather than having a tubular prop it was equipped with side wings which not only supported the shield but gave a modicum of protection to the user against enfilade. This plate was also much thicker, weighed about 23 kg, and could stop all small-arms fire with the exception of armour piercing rounds fired at very close range.

One other shield seen in photographs but as yet poorly documented was a small, curved plate with eye slits weighing about 6 kg, which was intended for use by snipers. Though reputed to have been possible to use strapped to the head, its weight and limited visibility make it seem much more practical as rudimentary cover for a prone rifleman. Many of the manlets existing today are painted field grey, but it is certain that they would have been suitably camouflage painted or disguised in the field.

Personal Equipment and Special Clothing

The German army began the war almost entirely reliant on leather for the fabrication of its personal equipment. The memoirs of more than one allied soldier described how the smell of damp leatherwork was one of the distinctive aromas which made up the instantly identifiable atmosphere of the German trenches and dugouts, along with cigars and coffee substitutes. It was questionable, however, whether leather equipments were as good as webbing: they became slippery when wet, could lose their resilience when dried out and were less good at spreading weight evenly. As the war progressed and supplies of leather became less and less adequate, long marching boots gave way to ankle boots, leather pouches and equipments were joined by canvas substitutes, and some straps were replaced by *Ersatz* or supplementary materials like woven paper.

The heart of the German personal equipment was the field belt, or *Feldkoppel* initially of brown leather for the majority of the troops, with black for *Jäger*. Later on, all belts were supposed to be black. The other ranks' belt was fastened with a plain metal buckle in the case of cavalry, the infantry having a plate embossed with a stylised crown motif encircled with the motto of their state. In the case of Prussia and Baden this was *Gott mit uns*; for the Bavarians *In Treue fest*; for the Saxons *Providentiae memor*, and for the Württembergers *Furchtlos und treu*. Pre-war belt buckles were usually well made and of a bimetallic construction, with a brass backing and a nickel centre. By 1916, stamped steel had become the norm and finally, by 1918, cheaper alloys were used. The belt was worn at the level of the lowest button on the jacket and was intended to rest in belt hooks which were an integral part of the *Waffenrock*. For 'walking out', black patent leather belts could be purchased, and senior NCOs in certain orders of dress would wear a sword suspended by means of a sling on the left side of the belt. Early on in the war, officers wore a separate pattern of belt known as the *Feldbinde* but in

1915 they were ordered to relinquish this in favour of a plain *Feldkoppel* of dark brown grained leather. At the same time, Adjutants were instructed to give up the wearing of their distinctive sashes.

Items commonly worn on the soldiers' belt included the bayonet frog with a decorative knot known as the *Troddel*, bread bag, entrenching tool, ammunition pouches, or pistol holster. For most of the

Bavarian mounted troops pictured in their field uniforms, 1914. They are armed with carbines and wear the small cavalry ammunition pouch sets with and without, leather supporting straps. Note the iron cross attached through the man's button hole. P. Hannon.

Above.

A selection of original *Troddeln*, or infantry bayonet knots, which identified the wearer's company. Left to right 8th, 10th, 2nd and 1st companies.

Left.

Front and rear view of a typical Model 1909 infantry ammunition pouch. This example was made at Ülm in 1910, of brown leather, though it appears to have been polished black during its service life. SB.

infantry, the bayonet knot was of various colour combinations allowing the distinguishing of one company of the regiment from another, but the *Jäger* knot was dark green, with silver stripes added for *Oberjäger* or corporals. The *Troddel* was very widely worn in 1914, but its use trailed off as the war continued. In theory each infantryman armed with a rifle should have carried a 1909 Model ammunition pouch or *Patronentasche* on either side of the belt. These pouches were of brown leather and both of the two units were divided into three smaller sections, each with its own little flap top which had a strap secured under the pouch. Each small section contained 20 cartridges, so the pair of pouches contained 120 rounds altogether. Mounted troops

Above and right.

The war economy grey canvas backpack, interior and exterior. This example is marked to the Prussian Guard Corps and dated 1915. The long bag was for tent accessories. MS, SB.

used a Model 1911 set of ammunition pouches, which were similar in design to those of the infantry but each compartment carried only ten rounds, thus it was that their belt equipment, when fully laden contained a total of 60 cartridges. Single ten-round carriers are also sometimes seen.

In practice there were severe shortages and many men, particularly in the reserves and *Landwehr*, had to make do with older patterns of ammunition pouch. At least three such types are seen in period photographs, but the commonest was the 1895 Model. Like the more modern pouches these were also worn as a pair either side of the belt and had a metal loop at the top to which the pack straps could be attached but, unlike them, each unit comprised a single rectangular leather box with a 45-round capacity. The 1895 Model pouches were initially of black leather, a hue calculated to match the dark blue or green dress uniforms current at the time of their inception. Model 1889 cartridge boxes were somewhat similar, and were again

Above.

Men of *Füsilier-Regiment Fürst Karl Anton von Hohenzollern (Hohenzollernsches)* Nr 40 equipped for the assault, early 1916.
***Pickelhauben* are worn with covers but no spikes. Two men with their backs to the camera are wearing an 'assault order' in which the shelter sheet is wrapped around the mess tin: cloth gas mask bags and water bottles are worn, whilst one man carries a pick and spare sand bags. On the left of the picture, grenade throwers are festooned with bombs, attached to the equipment by means of their belt hooks.**

Left.

A typical studio portrait of a *Landwehr* infantryman wearing the Model 1895 ammunition pouches. SB.

in black leather, but held only 30 rounds each. Smaller still was the Model 1887 cartridge box for non-commissioned officers; this was originally manufactured for the carriage of 11mm ammunition, but during the war was modified by the addition of spring clips to hold 15 rounds of modern 7.9 mm. A pair of 1887 NCO model pouches accommodated a total of only 30 rounds, even so they are frequently to be seen being worn by *Landwehr* troops.

The *Brotbeutel*, Model 1893, was the bread bag or small haversack in which the soldier customarily

Infantry on their way to the trenches of the Western Front. The majority wear a casual version of full marching order, with pack, folded greatcoat, ammunition pouches and gas mask tin. Both ankle boots and long marching boots are worn, rifles are slung around the neck and some men carry walking-sticks. IWM Q 88092.

Right.

Baden Landwehr Gefreiter Relling, pictured in a studio behind the Vosges sector, January 1915. His accoutrements include an *Alpenstock,* boots with puttees, a G 88 rifle and Model 1887 NCOs cartridge boxes, each of which held 15 rounds. Note the Baden helmet plate with *Landwehr* cross. *Gefreiter* Relling sent this picture home, expressing the wish that the war would soon be over and noting that the snow in the mountains lay 50 cm deep. SB.

carried his daily ration and very often a reserve supply of 30 rounds of ammunition, as well as his wire handled aluminium drinking cup. The bag varied in colour from the older reddish brown to wartime field grey, closed with a flap, and was normally carried on the right hip by means of three suspenders from the belt. The two outer straps terminated in buttoned tabs, and the centre one had a simple hook. When the

belt was not worn the bread bag could be carried by means of a leather strap over the shoulder. A loop and metal ring attached to the bread bag allowed the *Feldflasche* or service water bottle to be suspended from it.

The usual flask was the Model 1893, and consisted of an ovoid aluminium vessel with a flat back and a convex front, capable of containing one litre. Those water bottles made after about 1907 incorporated a screw thread closure, and are therefore sometimes accounted as a distinct model. The water bottle was originally covered in greyish brown felt. Later different fabric coverings were seen including field

Top left.

An early type bi-metal Prussian belt buckle, motto *Gott Mit Uns*; and a late type Bavarian buckle made from a one piece stamping with the wording *In Treue Fest*.

Below.

Men of Reserve Infantry Regiment Nr 215, pictured in Belgium, November 1914. Their equipment includes the Model 1889 cartridge boxes of black leather, which held 30 rounds each. Reserve infantry Regiment Nr 215 was a part of 46th Reserve Division: this formation was trained at Lockstedt camp north of Hamburg and was in action on the Yser in October and November 1914 suffering heavy casualties. SB.

grey and even brown corduroy. During the war the water bottle was also made in coated steel as well as aluminium. In certain 'assault orders', or when men did not expect to be relieved for some time, two water bottles were worn. Medical personnel often carried an outsize water bottle or *Labeflasche*, with drinking beaker and shoulder strap for use by the wounded.

When worn the entrenching tool or *Schanzzeug* was normally carried on the left hip. The entrenching tool consisted of a short spade with a wooden haft, the handle of which terminated in a ball finial. Its holder of brown, later black, leather encased the head and was suspended by means of two loops. It could be cross strapped securely to the bayonet sheath when in full marching order. On front line service the cutting edge was sometimes sharpened, for in the confines of a trench the entrenching tool could make a useful weapon. A smaller version of the entrenching tool, apparently intended for use by machine-gun troops, is also occasionally encountered. Within each battalion the majority were supposed to carry the entrenching tool, but a minority of 120 carried pickaxes (*Beilpiken*); and a further 60 were to be equipped with hatchets (*Beile*).

Communications troops using a field telephone in winter. Three of the men wear greatcoats and the senior NCO on the right is of sword carrying rank. IWM Q 114669.

The issue of tools to a company was 100 entrenching tools, ten picks and five hatchets. Larger shovels, picks, axes and saws were carried in the first line transport, or with supply train units.

The 1895 *Tornister* or back pack was an extremely distinctive piece of kit being made of cowhide, with the reddish brown hair surface still intact and a full length flap. It strapped over the shoulders in the normal way, but was also provided with straps by means of which it could also be attached to the ammunition pouches. When worn in this way it exerted an upward pressure on the pouches – straightening them out and preventing the sagging appearance sometimes seen when laden pouches were worn on the belt without the full equipment. The basic infantry *Tornister* was framed; between 29.5 cm and 33.5 cm in height, and 29 cm in width internally; and was lined with impermeable red-brown canvas. It was divided inside to provide: a compartment for clothes, or *Wäschebeutel*, for shirts, socks, handkerchiefs and drawers; two small pockets known as *Patronenbehälter*, for 15 cartridges each; a *Lebensmittelbeutel* or ration pocket; and a *Zeltzubehörbeutel*, or case for tent accessories. Dubbin or polish for the boots and leather equipment was often carried: there were many types, but one with particularly memorable advertising was known as

Stormtroops in a shell hole wearing an interesting version of 'assault order': grenade bags are slung around the shoulders and entrenching tools are worn high on the belt in improvised covers. The helmets have been crudely camouflaged with mud. IWM Q 23943.

'Frog's fat' – in reference to its supposed water repellent properties. Prussian *Jäger* wore an extraordinary pack at the outbreak of war, the *Dachs* (or Badger) Model 1895 / 97. This was basically of black leather or calf hide, but the back flap was of badger fur complete with the animal's face.

Later in the war, a plain field grey canvas economy version of the original backpack began to replace the cowhide models. This canvas backpack usually retained the leather shoulder straps and was trimmed with a thin strip of leather, strengthening its outer edge. Both the body of the pack and the straps normally bore makers' marks. Certain specialist troops, such as cyclists and mountain troops, used a rucksack rather than a backpack. Examples of these are encountered in both reddish brown, and grey canvas.

In full marching order the greatcoat and bivouac sheet were usually carried strapped around the top and sides of the pack, with the mess tin strapped to the back flap of the pack. The 1892 Model *Zeltbahn* or

bivouac sheet was of reddish brown canvas, but by the time war broke out was being replaced by a similar Model 1911 sheet of field grey. Two *Zeltbahnen* made up a complete tent, fastening by means of the buttons and button holes which ran around all four sides of each sheet. The tent half could also be used as a rain cape and to this end was provided with small loops through which a cord could be run to hold the sheet around the soldier's neck. The mess tin or *Kochgeshirr* Model 1910 could be of aluminium or steel and comprised two parts, each with its own handle. The deeper part could be used as a container for water, soups or stews, whilst the shallow lid section formed the frying pan. A combination fork and spoon Model 1910 was carried in the mess tin. The complete content of the pack in full marching order was supposed to comprise:

1 pair of trousers
1 forage cap or 'Mütze'
2 shirts
1 pair of socks
2 handkerchiefs
1 rice bag
1 'housewife' (containing needle and thread for kit repairs)

1 pair of drawers (underwear)
1 pair of shoe laces
1 set of boot brushes
1 grease tin
1 copper tin
1 salt bag
30 rounds of ammunition
1 canvas wallet containing: a tent pole *(Zeltstock)* in three sections; three tent pegs; one tent rope.

Food was usually provided in the form of a communally cooked field service ration or *Kriegsportion*, but it was usual for the soldier to carry three days of iron rations, the *Eiserner Bestand*, for use when normal mess facilities were not available. These iron rations totalled 750 g of biscuit; 600 g of preserved meat; 450 g of preserved vegetables; 75 g salt; and 75 g of coffee. In a single week the German army would demolish 30 million kilos of bread, 60 million kilos of potatoes and eight million kilos of meat. Bottled waters, beer, wine, brandy, tobacco and cigars were all popular in Germany, were frequently carried into the front line and were provided in small quantities with the official rations. As the war progressed, both foodstuffs and luxuries became ever scarcer and of inferior quality. By 1918, meats were issued in tiny quantities and there were meatless days – even bread and coffee were heavily bolstered with substitute materials. What could be had varied with time and locality: in 1916 the potato crop failed producing a 'turnip winter'; in Poland men of one division described how they survived on a diet of potatoes, carrots, radishes and pears.

The equipment with full pack, belt, food, tent, uniform, arms and allowance of 150 rounds of ammunition weighed about 55 lb. There was also a tendency for the burden to grow with time. As *Frontschwein* Private Wilhelm Schulin of Württemberg Grenadier Regiment Nr 119 observed in the midst of the filth and terror of the Somme, there was 'always more equipment, always something added: it is almost beastly the amount we have to carry'. Yet when well-fitted the complete equipment could be put on and taken off like a coat, without the need to unbuckle the pack from the belt, or the equipments from their hanging straps. Initially, German troops tended to assume either full marching order or a fighting order with belt and ammunition pouches but no pack, in the front line.

Very rapidly it was realised that this was insufficiently flexible for the various circumstances that were to be encountered in action. The result was not only the adoption of new pieces of equipment, like

bags for hand grenades hung round the neck and arm, or gas mask cases, but various 'assault' or *Stürmgepack* orders in which only a part of the full equipment was worn. One assault order which had a pre-war origin in training was the discarding of the main pack, but retaining the greatcoat tied around the body, with or without the mess tin attached to the greatcoat. Another alternative was to tie the *Zeltbahn* around the shoulder, and make do without the greatcoat. One or two field dressings, covered in grey fabric or unbleached drill material, might be sewn inside the front of the uniform jacket.

By the middle of the war a common method of stowage for the battlefield was to keep part or all of the belt kit, and wear the mess tin in the middle of the back. Around this was tied the tent section in a rough circle. As was described by Werner Beumelburg in February 1916, infantrymen sometimes wore: 'assault packs, overcoat and tent section in a horseshoe roll, haversack containing two days' fresh food and two emergency rations, one hundred and fifty cartridges in two pouches, two or three stick grenades, a bundle of empty earth sacks, an entrenching tool, a gas mask on the belt.' In yet another version of the assault order seen at Verdun the greatcoat was wrapped in the tent section and the whole tied to the back with the mess tin on the outside. Spades, grenades and empty sandbags were added as required using bread bag, pack and greatcoat straps to tie the various items securely together.

Special Clothing and Equipment

Since the German Army fought in every conceivable climate and terrain from the Carpathian mountains to southern Africa, it is hardly surprising that a significant variety of specialist garments and equipments were taken into use. What is perhaps more remarkable is that these varied so much in technological sophistication. At one end of the scale civilian waistcoats, cardigans, fur and leather coats, and scarves were a commonplace, at the other came very advanced concepts in combat equipment.

Ski Troops and Mountain Troops

Some of the most notable items were those used by the ski and mountain troops. Despite pre-war experiment, 1914 found these specialisms undeveloped: only after the outbreak of war did the call go out for the formation of a *Freiwilliges Skilaüferkorps*, or 'Volunteer Ski Corps'. The result was Bavarian *Schneeschuh Battalion Nr. 1*, officially incorporated in November 1914, under the command

NCO and private soldier of Bavarian Schneeschuh-Bataillon Nr 1 in action in the Vosges mountains, 1915.

First formed from volunteers in November 1914, the first Bavarian ski battalion was four companies strong: each company had one machine-gun and three rifle platoons, the total strength of the battalion being 27 officers and 619 men. A depot battalion was formed at Munich in December 1914. 'SB 1' was committed to action in the Vosges sector in January 1915 and was soon executing patrols deep into enemy territory. On 15 February, two companies of the regiment, advancing on skis, took the village of Hilsen by surprise and routed the French defenders. The success of the first ski unit led to the formation of a Prussian battalion for use on the Eastern Front and Württemberg companies which were soon deployed as *Gebirgsjäger,* or mountain rifles. The

of Major Alfred Steinitzer. Other units soon followed, Württemberg mountain rifles, mountain machine-gunners, and mountain artillery; eventually an *Alpenkorps* was formed in May 1915. Throughout the war German ski troops would remain distinctive, in terms both of their small unit tactics and their uniform.

The basic uniform of both ski and mountain units was the *Skilitewka* and *Berghosen* or *Skihosen*; essentially a loose fitting woollen jacket paired with

Alpenkorps was created in May 1915.

The NCO in the foreground wears the *Windjacke*, or 'wind jacket', a light thigh length snow camouflage garment over his pine green uniform. He carries a rucksack, climbing rope, binoculars and 1909 type ammunition pouches. His peaked *Skimütze* bears the Bavarian and the Reichs cockades on either side. The private on snow shoes wears the basic *Tannengrün* or pine green uniform of *Skilitewka* and *Skihose*, with goggles on his cap. No shoulder straps are worn on the jacket, but large 'S' motifs appear on the collar patches. He wears private purchase gloves; the issue version were of grey and white reversible cloth. The men in the background, using their ski poles as rests for their carbines, are wearing the full snow camouflage kit of hooded *Windbluse* and *Windhose*. This suit was made of water repellent cotton; white on one side and brownish green on the other. Painting by Christa Hook.

either 'mountain' or 'ski' trousers. Unlike the rest of the army this uniform was *Tannengrün* or 'pine green' in colour. The *Skilitewka* bore a resemblance to the contemporary hunting jacket, being fly fronted with pleated chest pockets with buttoned flaps slanting inward toward the breast bone, and hip pockets cut on the opposite slant also with buttoned flaps. A large fifth pocket was incorporated on the lower back, closed by means of a vertical flap at either side, each flap having two buttons. There were no shoulder straps except for officers, and the collar was of the stand and fall variety. On the green piped collar appeared the distinctive specialist insignia, an 'S' embroidered in green on a large collar patch or, in the case of Württemberg, smaller green oblong collar patches ornamented with a button. Württemberg troops were also notable for their green *Schulterwülster* or wings, which were practical as well as decorative since they served to hold the equipment straps in place. The cuffs of the *Skilitewka* were fitted with small buttoned tabs which allowed the garment to be tightened at the wrist so as to keep out the weather. The coat was lined grey.

The basic *Skihosen*, or ski trousers, were straight legged, piped green and high waisted at the back where a half belt and buckle arrangement could be used to tighten them. A shortened modified

A *Gebirgs*, or mountain, *Jäger* in an evocative studio portrait c.1915. The grey-green *Waffenrock* is worn with Swedish cuffs and green piping, but no shoulder straps. The cap has a protective cover and metal shod ankle boots are worn with puttees. The equipment includes the bread bag and pack or rucksack stowed with spare footwear, mess tin and tent sheet. The weapon is the 7.92 mm, *Karabiner AZ*.
P. Hannon.

Above.

Crown Prince Wilhelm, commander of the Fifth Army during a visit to the front. The Crown Prince wears a hussar officers cap, breeches, lace up boots with gaiters and a non-regulation leather jacket with officer's shoulder boards. The stretcher bearer with whom he is in conversation is distinguished by a red cross arm band. Note the other officers of the entourage who wear both the *Waffenrock* **and** *Bluse* **type uniforms as well as a variety of headgear.** IWM Q 23744.

Left.

A *Feldwebel* **of mountain mortar company 194. Rank is distinguished by the lace on the points of the jacket collar, large collar buttons and two bars of lace on the Swedish cuffs. This grade of NCO is a** *Portepee* **rank, meaning that the holder is entitled to carry an officer's sword and knot. The sword is carried for the sake of this studio portrait, but is unlikely to have been taken into action. Note also the** *Minenwerfer* **unit badge on the left upper arm; the** *Edelweiss* **mountain troops device on the side of the cap; the marksman's lanyard; the puttees;** *Alpenstock***; and the company document wallet stuffed into the jacket front.** P. Hannon.

'knickerbocker' version of the trousers was also worn, apparently mainly by machine-gunners, with buttons at the knee to hold up long thick socks. These

A stormtroop company, 1918. About half the men are equipped with grenade bags, and three officers in soft peaked caps carrying binoculars are visible towards the right of the group. The main firepower is two MG 08, and one MG 08/15 light machine gun, shown foreground centre. Both MG 08 weapons have barrel armour and one of the crewmen is equipped with dragging straps. IWM Q 55371.

A man of 2. Garde-Schützen Bataillon in an odd mixture of practical combat clothing and walking out dress, pictured in May 1916. The ankle boots and leather reinforced Berghosen in particular are likely to be indicative of hard service. This unit was attached to 12 Landwehr Division in Alsace for much of 1915 and 1916, where heavy casualties were taken in battle on the Hartmannswillerkopf. In September 1916 the 2. Garde Schützen were sent to Macedonia. P. Hannon.

breeches were sometimes also worn with leather or cloth reinforcements, in which case they were commonly known as *Berghosen*, literally 'mountain' or climbing trousers. Usually puttees were worn, together with hobnailed boots which were also reinforced with irons around the edge of the sole. Some photographs show what appears to be dark collarless woollen shirts and sweaters being worn as warm layers under the pine green uniform.

The headgear for the mountain ensemble was the *Skimütze* a soft pine green peaked cap, inspired by similar Norwegian and Austrian hats. It was piped green around the crown, and was equipped with a fold down flap which was secured in front by means of a pair of horn or metal buttons. Initially the cap was worn with cockades mounted rather incongruously on either side; the Reichs cockade on the right and the state cockade on the left. Later these cockades were moved to the front of the cap, one high on the front, the other between the buttons of the flap.

Mountain units often wore a distinctive Edelweiss badge on the left hand side of the headgear. According to *Handbook of the German Army*, the Alpine Korps and 200th Division also wore a special badge above the upper cockade of the cap. This was described as being of metal 'representing a stag's antlers with a sword and pine branches and the motto *Karpathian Korps* on a scroll'. This could only reasonably have been worn from 1916 when the units were deployed to the relevant area.

Perhaps the most innovative parts of the mountain uniform were the camouflage and protective garments which could be worn over the basic jacket and trousers. The *Windjacke* was a short reversible coat of cotton, stone grey on one side, white on the other, fastened by means of eight horn buttons and hooks at the collar. Drawstrings were used to tighten the cuffs and bottom of the coat and buttoned hip pockets were provided. The *Windjacke* was most commonly, though not exclusively, worn by the officers and non-commissioned officers. The *Windbluse* was a bulkier garment intended to be an outer layer, and was a hooded, wind proof, water resistant, short coat. It, too, was reversible, white on one side, brown-green on the other, and was sometimes distinguished by a black 'S' embroidered on the left sleeve. For the legs, *Windhose* or *Überhose* were worn: these overalls could be wrapped around the calf, tightening the lower leg to facilitate skiiing and climbing. White camouflage covers were also made for the cap and rucksack, and in especially inhospitable conditions, canvas over boots and grey greatcoats were also worn. Issue gloves for ski troops were made of cloth and reversible, grey one side, white the other.

As might be expected, skis of various lengths were used: initially volunteers were allowed to use their own, but later standard issues were made. These were longer for flatter terrain where long distance cross-country work was to be expected, shorter where wooded slopes were likely to be encountered. *Schneereiten* or snow shoes of several different types

The uniforms of the *Schutztruppen* from an inter-war cigarette card series. Top row, left to right: a trumpeter of the South West Africa *Schutztruppen* in the grey walking out dress as worn at home in Germany; an *Unteroffizier* of the South West Africa force in greatcoat; and a *Leutnant* of the same force in the *Kord* or corduroy *Feldrock*. Centre row, left to right; an adjutant of the South West Africa *Schutztruppen* in service dress; a sergeant of the East Africa *Schutztruppen* in the khaki brown Feldrock; and a coloured *Unteroffizier* signaller of the East Africa *Schutztruppen* with heliograph. Bottom row, left to right; a native soldier of the Cameroon force wearing the distinctive *Kamerun* cap; a *Hauptman* of the Cameroon force in the white tropical uniform; and bottom right a Marine *Gefreiter* of the East Asiatic detachment wearing the *Braundrell* or brown drill uniform with *Tropenhelm*. S.B . & M.S.

were also in use, as were large tents and sledges. There was also a stretcher sledge for casualties.

Stormtroops

The connection between the clothing and equipment worn by mountain and ski troops, and that worn by assault troops and Stormtroops later in the war, has been widely commented, yet this influence was only part of the story. In every war which lasted for years rather than months, German forces of the 19th and 20th centuries have moved from more fitted formal clothing to simpler, looser, and more practical styles. The Wars of Liberation against Napoleon had seen the widespread use of the *Litewka*, green, and grey clothing, waterproof garments, and practical rather than decorative caps for field service. The Second World War would likewise see the German army move from a detailed and well-fitting service dress, first to a simplified style, and later to a suit which approximated to 'battledress', with many new pieces of specialised clothing and a 'ski' cap.

It is also worth bearing in mind that 'assault parties', 'assault battalions', and eventually 'assault divisions' were formed during the First World War. The intention was not primarily to create an elite, but to pass on new methods of fighting, equipment and tactics to as much of the army as possible. It is arguable, therefore, whether leather-reinforced trousers, grenade bags, ankle boots and the like should be seen specifically as 'stormtroop' items, or merely as the sign of recently experienced combat personnel. Indeed it is true that as early as 1915 'hand-grenade troops' and 'assault squads' had been formed from within existing regiments. These integrated groups, equipped with more than one type of weapon, were intended to attack the enemy trenches in scattered knots rather than with advances in linear

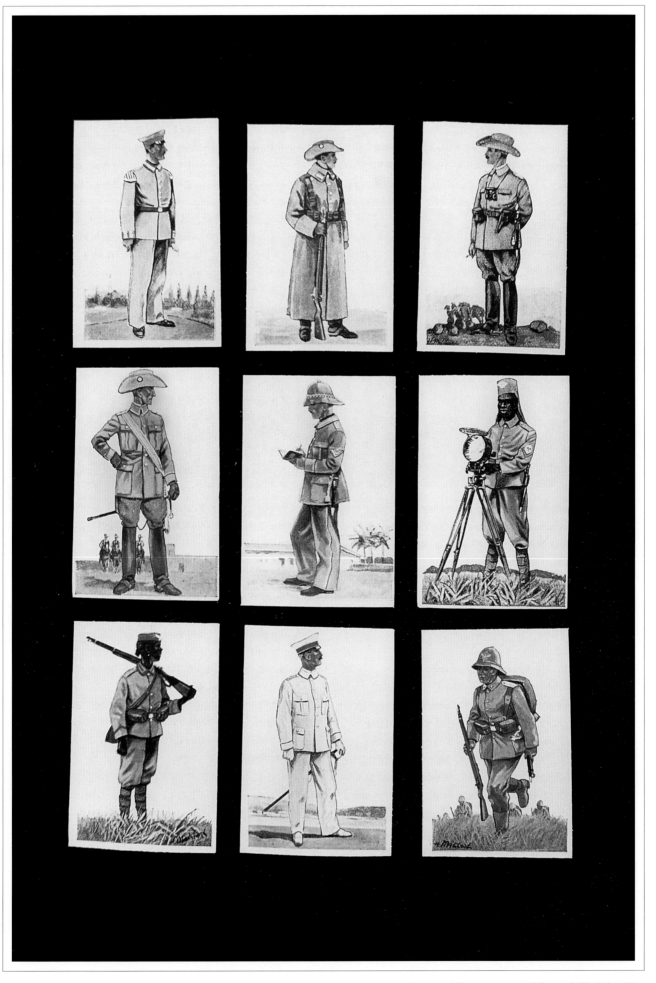

Men of *Infanterie-Regiment Prinz Louis Ferdinand von Preußen (2. Magdeburgisches) Nr 27* in the trenches near Arras. Greatcoats and scarves are worn as are large wooden sabots filled with insulating straw. IWM Q 51079.

formation with the rifle. The advent of 'stormtroop' tactics was thus a developmental process which took two or three years, rather than appearing out of the blue in the last year of war.

Thus it was that the best known of the 'stormtroop' formations were essentially of an experimental or training nature. *Sturmabteilung Kalsow* for example was first formed in 1915 and initially served to demonstrate the use of 37 mm cannon in the attack. After being renamed after its new commander Willy Rohr, the same unit went on to experiment widely with flamethrowers, light machine-guns, steel helmets and light mortars. Subsequently new *Sturmbataillone* were formed for each army, primarily to teach the new *Stosstrupptaktik* or assault tactics more widely, turning troops of ordinary regiments into Stormtroops.

Until early 1917 the uniforms of the *Sturmbataillone* were mixed indeed, their personnel having been drawn not only from *Jäger* units, but widely from throughout the army. In February and

March of that year new orders were issued that infantry uniform was to be worn by the majority of the men, trench mortar crews being dressed as pioneers, and gun crews as artillery. Shoulder straps were to be marked with the number of the *Sturmbataillone*. Mortar *Kompanie* were to have black shoulder straps with a number and 'MW' in red; the gun battery personnel were to have red shoulder straps with a grenade and the number of their unit in yellow. The exceptions to the general rule were Rohr's *Sturmbataillone* which was to be dressed as pioneers, and the *Jäger Sturmbataillone* which kept *Jäger* distinctions.

Trench Raiders

For raiding purposes, light equipment with a maximum of close combat weaponry was the norm, the precise nature of which varied slightly with time and place. According to orders issued to *Reserve Infanterie Regiment Nr 110* for a raid against the British near La Boiselle in April 1916 the dress was 'attack order without greatcoat or cap, belts to be worn without pouches, gas masks to be worn and tucked into the tunic'. The raiders were armed with a mixture of rifles, pistols, and grenades and also carried wire cutters. For

German and British infantry during the Christmas fraternisation of 1914. The man smoking wears the *Pickelhaube* with cover and greatcoat with scarlet collar patches, but no shoulder straps. The man next to him wears the toque with the *Feldmütze* over the top. IWM Q 70075.

identification purposes a triangle of white linen was sewn onto the breast and back of the uniform.

A notebook taken from a *Feldwebel* of *Reserve-Infanterie* Regiment Nr 261 in the spring of 1917 advised some variations on the theme. This recommended that 'white brassards' were impractical due to their visibility and that caps were preferable to steel helmets. Suggested equipment for raiding included a pistol on a lanyard around the neck, torches, Very pistols, daggers and trench clubs but raiders were told to remove all identifying marks and documents. Charges were to be carried for blowing in enemy dug-outs, and tent sections kept handy to help carry the wounded and any captured booty.

Kriegsgefangene - Prisoners

One other special purpose set of clothing should not be ignored - that worn when the German soldier became a prisoner. Obviously this varied depending

when and where he was taken, and in some instances men had to survive indefinitely in the uniform in which they were captured, but the dress adopted by Germans who were held prisoner of war in England has been well recorded. As was decreed in the *Vorschriften Für Kriegsgefangene*, on no account were prisoners allowed to have ordinary civilian clothes. What they were to wear according to regulation was laid down in a document entitled *Prisoner of War Companies, Orders and Instructions* of February 1918. This specified that German prisoners first arriving at an 'Army Transit Cage' could be provided with a greatcoat, mess tin, soap and a towel; this modest provision was expected to last until the uniform worn at the time of capture was worn out.

Thereafter they were issued with a special outfit. This comprised a jacket and trousers of 'brown courduroy', with circular patches of blue cloth. On the back of the tunic and greatcoat three inch numerals in red cloth were to be sewn by company tailors, giving the prisoner's number. The matching cap was to have a blue band, and be 'similar in shape to that used by the German Army' but the prisoners were expected to make up their own headgear from material provided. A cardigan was issued during the winter months and, if they were not already in possession of them, they were

An artillery officer c. 1916 wearing a special lightweight summer version of the field uniform with patch pockets, eight buttons and rank boards. Note the breeches and ankle boots. SB.

A well-known photograph of a soldier throwing a stick grenade during Stormtroop training at Sedan. He wears ankle boots and puttees and is equipped with a grenade bag and the soft early type gas mask container.

also to receive a pair of 'part worn' refurbished boots, a haversack, two pairs of flannel drawers, a woollen vest, two flannel shirts, two pairs of socks, a waterproof sheet, blanket and other small 'necessaries'. All items of clothing were to be stamped with the prisoner's serial number in numerals two inches tall. 'Dungaree suits' could be issued to prisoner of war cooks. Interestingly the Imperial War Museum collection contains a prisoner's cap similar in general shape to the ordinary peakless issue *Mütze*. This is made of mid-grey serge overall, and entirely devoid of insignia. It was manufactured in Leeds in 1918, but whether it was made using prisoner labour is not recorded.

Gustav Ebelshauser of Bavarian Regiment Nr 17, held at Bramley near Basingstoke, recorded a variation on the prisoner uniform and noted that the prisoners called themselves 'the men in brown' due to the colour of their new suits: 'No objection could be raised as to the quality of the material - a Manchester tweed of extra strength and durability. The coat closed at the neck with an inch high collar, but without stiffness.

There was no vest [waistcoat]. Pants and coats matched. Blue Moon was one of the preferred nicknames by which the prisoners designated their suits. A perfect circle had been cut out of the back of each coat. To cover this large round hole a piece of blue fabric of different material had been sewn in. The same procedure had been followed for the making of the pants. Only the blue patch, instead of being round, was shaped oval and appeared on the front of one of the legs. Thanks to this deliberate disfigurement of the suit a prisoner could be recognised both ways, coming and going.'

Perhaps surprisingly the old field grey at Bramley was patched, preserved, cleaned and worn when the Bavarian prisoners returned to Germany in 1919.

Colonial Troops

Germany's relative lack of colonial possessions and a 'place in the sun' were amongst the reasons that she went to war in 1914. Nevertheless she did have

'A souvenir of the World War 1914–1915'. Soldiers in a typical mixture of fatigue and civilian dress prepare to tap a barrel of beer behind the lines. SB.

The mosquito was a particular hazard of the Eastern Front. This infantryman wears a mosquito net over the *Pickelhaube*; his weapon is a captured Russian Moisin-Nagant rifle. IWM Q 29956.

significant holdings in Africa, and these were protected by the local *Schutztruppen* or defence forces. These troops were originally raised under the authority of the *Reichskommissar* in the period 1889 to 1891 and were subsequently taken into Imperial service. Surprisingly few personnel were involved and the majority of these were natives, sometimes referred to as *Farbige*, meaning literally 'coloured'. Very often native troops formed the bulk of the rank and file, with white non-commissioned and commissioned officers.

So it was that prior to the war, German East Africa (*Deutsch-Ostafrika*); German South West Africa (*Deutsch-Südwestafrika*); and the Cameroons (*Kamerun*) each had their own small garrison. The East African forces had their headquarters, recruit depot, signal section and one company at Dar-es-Salaam with a further 13 companies dotted around the country from Lindi on the east coast to Ujiji in the west. In 1914, the *Ostafrika Schutztruppen* numbered fewer than 3,000 of whom a mere one in ten were Europeans – white officials, engineers, NCOs, officers and medical

staff. In the Cameroons there were 12 similar companies totalling just under 2,000 men with their headquarters at Soppo and an artillery detachment at Duala.

In South West Africa, there were two commands, the northern, based on Windhoek and a southern at Keetmanshoop. The northern part comprised three companies, including a machine-gun company, plus an artillery battery and various hospital, transport and depot sections. The southern part had similar administrative and support facilities and two batteries; it also had six companies including a *Kamelreiter* or Camel Corps, and machine-gun sections. Even so the South West Africa forces were only a little more numerous than elsewhere, with 2,000 Europeans on the strength. In addition to the above the German colonies had small numbers of *Polizeitruppen*: paramilitary local police troops. These were based not only in the Cameroons, East, and South West Africa, but in Togo, the South Seas and a handful in China.

From 1896 a common uniform was introduced across the various *Schutztruppen*. For Europeans this uniform was of two basic types, a 'home service' dress and a field dress used on active service in the colonies. The home service dress was of light grey cloth with a stand and fall collar, Swedish cuffs, shoulder straps and piping. For East Africa the pipings were white, in South West Africa light blue, and in the Cameroons, red. The trousers were light grey, and the headgear was a form of grey slouch hat turned up at the right side and a cockade in the Imperial black, white, red colours on the upturned flap. White *Litzen* were worn by other ranks, with silver for officers, the centre line of both being red. The leather equipment was brown. Additionally officers were entitled to the use of a formal neat white drill uniform, with four flapped patch pockets on the jacket and a white peaked service cap with appropriately coloured band.

The usual field uniform jacket for Europeans was of brownish khaki drill with four patch pockets, white metal buttons, shoulder straps, turn down collar, simple turn back cuffs and the relevant piping but no *Litzen*. A rare surviving other ranks example in the Imperial War Museum collection has the blue South West Africa piping down the centre, and around the cuffs and collar with pleated breast pockets which are cut so as to slope downwards towards the centre closure. The buttons bear the Prussian crown and the shoulder straps are of red, white and black twisted cord.

The trousers for the field uniform were of matching khaki. The headgear was a lightweight khaki tropical helmet, or *Tropenhelm*, with the Imperial cockade on the front. Grey corduroy field uniforms and slouch hats were also sometimes worn on active service. Leather service equipment was again brown and included a unique set of ammunition pouches worn on a belt with shoulder braces. The native troops wore khaki drill, the jacket having white metal buttons and turn down collar, and greyish blue puttees. Headgear for native troops appears to have varied, with a khaki fez with neck curtain being the commonest, but a form of turban was also worn. In the Cameroons the native headgear was a peakless red felt cap with a central tassle of blue and an eagle badge worn on the front.

It is interesting to note that after the war Germany was denuded of her colonial possessions. Thus it was that masses of 'brown' uniforms were surplus to requirements. Not long afterwards the tropical shirts were put to use by extremist political organisations and the result was the first clothing of the inter-war 'Brown shirts'.

Other Warm Weather Uniforms

German forces also took the field in Palestine, Bulgaria and Greece, under conditions which were warm enough to warrant the issue of special clothing. In all these theatres it appears that a mixture of the normal field grey and khaki drill was worn, usually with grey or brown puttees and ankle boots. The khaki uniforms were generally of a four pocket design, with turn down collars and shoulder straps which were sometimes embroidered with red numerals.

Headgear varied both with time and specific theatre. In Palestine the colonial *Tropenhelm* with Imperial cockade was worn at the outset, but both its relative impracticality and its resemblance to British headgear meant that it was later abandoned and replaced by peaked caps of brown drill, with or without a neck curtain. Elsewhere grey felt *Pickelhauben*, sometimes with covers, were worn prior to the introduction of steel helmets; lance caps similarly were given khaki covers and neck curtains in hot climates.

Perhaps surprisingly warm weather clothing also made reasonably frequent appearances during the summer on the Eastern Front, and possibly to a limited extent in the west. The most common manifestations were lightweight versions of the field service uniform in light field grey, usually worn by officers and senior non-commissioned officers. The 'summer' jackets of linen or cotton varied considerably in detail. Broadly speaking they were either with eight buttons exposed down the front and shoulder straps, in an approximation of the *Waffenrock*, or with a fly front, but unlike the *Waffenrock* or *Bluse* they normally had four pockets. Beyond this it is difficult to generalise since garments have been observed both without cuffs, and with turnbacks. Although button down pocket flaps were worn, the detail of pockets also varied, some being plain patches with rounded flaps, others pleated with shaped flaps.

Weapons

Rifles

Throughout the war the majority of German troops were equipped with rifles, and the vast bulk of these rifles were Mauser types. Wilhelm and Peter Paul Mauser, born in 1834 and 1838 respectively, were the 11th and 13th children of a 'parts filer' working at the Royal Württemberg rifle factory at Oberndorf am Neckar, and they themselves commenced working in the factory at the age of 12. From the early 1860s, the brothers began to design firearms of their own, but meeting with little success in their own country moved to Liege where they eventually perfected the model 1871 bolt action infantry rifle. This weapon combined the Mausers' own breech mechanism with a barrel and rifling akin to the famed French Chassepot, a trigger mechanism of the type already in use in the Dryse needle gun and a cartridge developed at the arsenal at Spandau. Despite its varied provenance, the single-shot model 1871 offered considerable advantages over what had gone before, since it was possible to load and cock the weapon in one action simply by opening and closing the bolt. The rifle made the Mauser brothers' reputation.

Over the next decade continual minor improvements in design would follow. The model 1871/74 repeater with eight-round magazine superseded the original model. This in its turn was succeeded in German service by a model 1888 hybrid Mauser-Mannlicher, responsibility for which fell to the official rifle test commission or *Gewehr Prüfungs* Commission. It was not long however before the G 88 was itself deemed ready for revision as weaknesses were becoming apparent. One of these was that under certain circumstances it proved possible to load two cartridges simultaneously, and as one round was forced in behind the other a premature explosion was sometimes the result. The G 88 also experienced rapid barrel wear and at best this led to inaccuracy, at worst to barrel ruptures. Every possible explanation was put forward from simple design flaws, to problems in the relationship between bullet calibre and bore size, to 'Jewish conspiracy'.

Whatever the real root of the problem it was all too clear that if accidents were to be avoided the service life of the G 88 should be a short one. Fresh trials began in 1895, and amongst the choices considered were the Mauser 8 mm model 88/97, and an experimental small calibre rifle. The third major option was a hybrid, taking together the best elements of preceding designs, and with hardly anything novel added. In the event this safety first approach prevailed, and the weapon which the Kaiser would eventually designate the 'rifle 98', or G 98, on 5th April 1898, proved to be an outstandingly successful compromise.

The G 98 chambered the same 7.92 mm round as the old G 88, massive stocks of which remained to be used, and the new rifle was operated by means of the Mauser mechanism self-cocking breech. The barrel was long at 74 cm and the integral magazine had a five round capacity being filled from a charger. To load, the bolt was pulled back to its fullest extent and a charger placed in the guides over the magazine plate and pushed down. The cartridges were thus stripped from the charger down into the magazine. The bolt was closed, leaving the mechanism cocked and the first cartridge in the chamber. The rifle was now ready to shoot. The sights were of a distinctive 'ramp' type, of the so-called 'Lange' system invented by Lieutenant Colonel Lange, director of the ammunition factory at Spandau and already utilised on the model 88/97 rifle (as seen on the G 98 these were at first graduated from 200 to 2,000 metres). The rifle stock was elegant and elongated, but perhaps more importantly was fitted with a pistol style grip. In the butt was a small, circular metal insert on which could be stamped unit markings. Pre-war each gun cost 54 Marks, of which one Mark went to Mauser by way of royalty.

A large number of types of bayonet would

eventually be used with the G 98, including many war time production *Ersatz* models, obsolete types and private purchase variations. There were perhaps five reasonably standard varieties which may be categorised as follows. The '*Seitengewehr* S98' was the original bayonet designed for the weapon with a thin blade 52 cm long; it was also produced in saw back variations. The S98/02 was a saw back for the pioneers, and the KS 98, or short model 98, was originally intended for machinegunners, and was only 25 cm long. The S98/05 was perhaps the best known of the group, for although just 37 cm in length, it had a very broad blade and a wicked appearance which has prompted some to christen it the 'butcher' bayonet. Late versions of this again included a saw back option. From 1915 onwards appeared the S84/98 new model, a short 25 cm bayonet which would last until the Second World War.

Mass production of the new rifle began in 1900, the major manufacturers being the Prussian state arsenals of Danzig, Erfurt and Spandau, which were later joined by the Mauser factory itself. First issues went to the Navy, the Guards and the *Ostasiatisches Expeditionkorps*, or East Asia Expeditionary force, which was sent to China in the wake of the Boxer rebellion. The Prussian army corps began re-equipment thereafter, and about three corps were

completed yearly from then onwards. Bavarian production at Amberg commenced in 1903, and the Bavarian army corps were equipped by 1907. Not all second line troops had received the rifle even by 1914.

One significant hiccup occurred during the process, for by the early years of the 20th century the old *Patronen 88* cartridge with its rounded nose and *Blattchen-Pulver* Type 426 propellant was showing its age. Experiment showed that a pointed bullet, or *Spitzgeschoss*, with a new *Spandauer* powder gave much better performance. The rifles already made were therefore converted to take a new 'S' type round, and new production was later altered to suit the new ammunition. With practice, conversion of the rifles made for the old round became a very slick process indeed, taking only four minutes.

One drawback of the new cartridge was that it made nonsense of the sighting arrangement because the 'S' bullet was more powerful and maintained a relatively flat trajectory out to 400 metres. Two modifications to the *Lange* sights were therefore made: first the 200 and 300 metre settings were deleted; then, because the G 98 now tended to shoot high at really close ranges a simple *hilfskorn* or auxiliary sight was developed. These matters dealt with, the G 98 went on to become an exceptionally successful weapon – very accurate to long ranges, reliable and reasonably soldier proof.

Though good, the G 98 did have certain disadvantages, particularly in comparison with the British Short Magazine Lee Enfield which it would

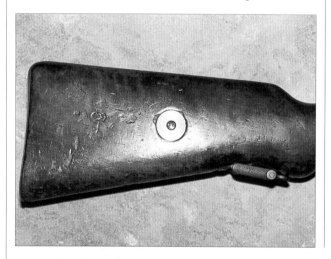

Left.

The stock of the G 98, showing not only the inspector's marks but the butt disc on which appeared unit identification marks, in this case II S.B. or second 'Sea Battalion'.

Below.

The G 98 seen here with bolt fully retracted and an example of the vicious looking 1905 model bayonet. Notice the large *Lange* ramp type sight.

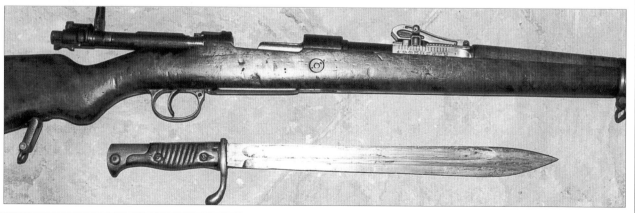

Above.

Men of *Magdeburgisches Infanterie Regiment Nr 67* prepare to march, including fifth from left back row, Hans Hollender, September 1914. Most of the men are now clad in the field grey service uniforms as adopted in 1910, their *Pickelhauben* worn with cloth covers with the regimental number. The group includes two NCOs in peaked caps, one of whom carries a sword. The G 98 rifles are piled in pyramids of four by means of linking together their under barrel cleaning rods. The not very legible placard centre includes three intelligible words *Auf Nach Paris*: 'on to Paris!'. SB.

Right.

The obsolete G 88 Mauser in the hands of a *Landwehr* man or Reservist.

face in the trenches. First was its length which, though commensurate with accurate shooting and with bayonet fighting, was unwieldy in a small space. The trenches obviously were confined spaces, and moreover there was little bayonet fighting and not much long range shooting. Secondly, the five round magazine, whilst perfectly adequate in a sniping or target shooting role, was not capacious enough in any rapid fire situation. Finally, and perhaps most significantly the G 98 could not compete on an even

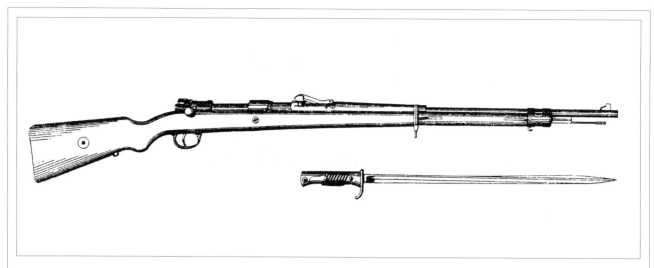

Line drawing of the G 98 with its long bladed S 98 bayonet, as depicted in *Text Book of Small Arms* of 1904.

footing with the SMLE on grounds of sheer volume of fire. The difference was apparently marginal, but significant.

Various solutions to these problems, each of which was minor taken individually, were sought as the Great War progressed. The short *Karabiner* 98a was already on issue to cavalry and certain other troops, and more short rifles were introduced in order to overcome problems associated with length. Carbines therefore became a distinctive feature of the ski troops and stormtroops. A more dramatic remedy was applied to the G 98 itself to address the inadequate ammunition capacity. This was the addition of a 25 round 'trench' magazine which brought the magazine space up to more than twice that enjoyed by the Enfield. However this *Mehr- lader*, literally a 'more loader', never seems to have been produced in sufficient quantities for general issue, and whilst most military museum collections in Britain can boast at

The G 98 with trench magazine or *Mehrlader*. Also visible on this example are a large bolt cover and a muzzle cover, both useful additions to the basic equipment in the filth of the trenches.

least one G 98, the large magazine variants are few and far between. In 1918, therefore, work had begun on a *Mauser-Gewehr* 18, or *Mauser Schützengraben und Nahkampfgewehr*, literally translated as a 'Mauser Trench and close combat rifle'. This weapon was intended to be short, and have a magazine capacity up to 25 rounds; but development of the Bergman submachinegun and the end of the war rendered the project obsolete.

A less serious alteration brought into existence the *Stern-Gewehr*, or 'star rifle' version of the G 98, in 1916. This weapon, marked with a small star on the chamber, was the natural effect of expanded production and a fall in manufacturing values. As a result of overwhelming demand, which had left quite significant segments of the forces armed with obsolete or captured rifles like the G 88 and Moisin Nagant, it was decided to increase production of various components of the standard infantry rifle by bringing in smaller metal working companies. The parts they made were delivered to the government arsenals, and from them were assembled new rifles. Since there was no guarantee that these extra parts would fit on rifles other than those to which they were originally assembled a distinctive mark was required, hence the star. One other minor emergency measure was the substitution of the expensive and time-consuming,

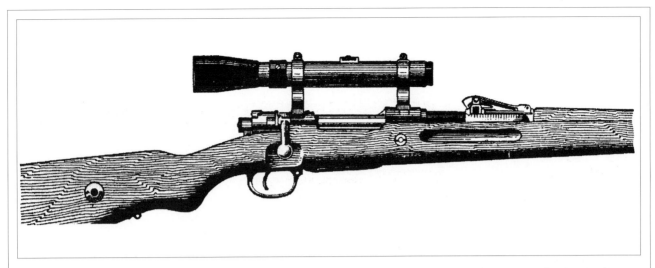

The *Scharfschützen Gewehr 98* with its turned down bolt handle and sniper scope.

seasoned walnut stocks and hand-guards with cheaper alternatives such as copper beech and glued two piece constructions which used up pieces of wood which by themselves, were too small. Interesting though small-scale modifications for special purposes also included luminous sights for use in poor light, and a *Gewehr mit Spiegelkolben* or rifle with periscope mirror, for firing out of a trench without showing one's head.

Snipers and Marksmen

The G 98 was widely adopted as a sniper's weapon, and its range, accuracy and power were well suited to the role. In 1914 it was ordered that 15,000 standard manufacture G 98s be retrofitted with Goerz *Certar Kurz* telescopic sights, but since the demand for sniper weapons was far greater than the potential supply of standard military arms, hunting weapons of various types were taken into service. These had Mauser mechanisms, usually fired the old *Patrone* 88, and were fitted with commercial sights. They were initially donated by the public and, after January 1915, were requisitioned for the purpose. Binoculars by Zeiss, Goerz and others were also issued to sniper and observer teams. Many of these were of the official *Fernglas 08* pattern. These early efforts, and the presence of many huntsmen and game keepers in the ranks paid dividends, giving the German army an initial upper hand in the sniping war in the west – a lead which was to be maintained for over a year. In the east a permanent superiority was gained over the Russians.

Very soon a dedicated sniper rifle was under manufacture. This modified arm was known as the *Scharfschützen Gewehr 98* or literally 'Sharpshooters model 98 rifle'. In essence this was a basic G 98,

picked from the production line as a flawless and accurate example, then finished to better than normal standards, and fitted with a bolt handle which bent down to a less awkward position than the usual right angle. A four times magnification Goerz or Zeiss telescope was mounted; in the Prussian instance this was often off-set to the left so that the magazine could still be loaded using a charger, whilst the Bavarians favoured a scope set directly over the bore. Issues were also made of special 'K' type ammunition with a steel core capable of penetrating metal shields and cover impervious to the normal lead cored bullet.

Detail of specialist sniper clothing is elusive though there is reference to painted canvas and burlap robes, and to head veils which would have assisted with concealment. As the British intelligence document *Summary of Recent Information Regarding the German Army and its Methods* observed in January 1917, 'snipers have been discovered wearing uniforms made of sandbags, merging themselves with the parapet'; scruffy and irregular fronts to the trenches helped make them even less visible. Telescopic sights were often carried in a special case suspended from the belt when not in use and these tubes were variously of leather, metal, or even cardboard with a canvas cover. The scopes themselves were usually blued or painted in a textured olive green, rendering them less obvious.

Specific sniper insignia appears rarely to have been worn, but one document refers to a 'special badge of two crossed oak leaves above the upper badge of the cap'. The much more frequently encountered ordinary marksman's distinction was the *Schützenschnur*, which had been introduced in 1894. This was a plaited cord or lanyard in the black, white and red Imperial colours which hung from the shoulder to the top button of the tunic. It came in eight grades. The first three were made of wool, with the addition of one, two or three acorns according to class. The fourth grade was of silk, with no acorns, but silver replaced the white. The fifth

The MG 08 on its sledge mount with crew. The ammunition is contained in 1915 type metal boxes, each one of which carried a 250 round belt. Note how two such boxes can be carried together in one hand. The NCO in charge wears a pistol holster and has a uniform with collar and cuff *Litzen*. That this is very much a posed picture is emphasised by the fact that the loader offers up an empty ammunition belt! M. Pegler.

grade was much as the fourth but had a crowned medallion in yellow metal added; the last three grades were as the fifth with the addition of one, two or three acorns.

'Emperor' shooting badges were also awarded for wear on the upper arm of dress uniforms. These *Kaiser-Abzeichen* were dated by year, and topped by a crown, but varied in pattern according to the arm of service to which the winner belonged. The infantry badge showed crossed rifles within leaves, the *Jäger* badge showed a stag's head, and the artillery badge crossed gun barrels and leaves.

It is interesting that operational orders specified that sniper weapons should be issued only to 'qualified marksmen who can assure results when firing from trench to trench, and especially at dusk or during clear nights when ordinary weapons are not satisfactory'. Shots were to be taken with discretion, not as part of

general suppressive fire, and snipers were to be allowed to move away from their parent unit in order to secure the best field of fire. Where possible a notebook was kept of the positions of enemy riflemen and vulnerable points.

Machine Guns

Germany began experimenting with machine guns as early as 1888 when the Kaiser purchased a number of 'World Standard' 11 mm Maxim machine guns for his Guard Dragoon regiments, but it was not until the turn of the century that such weapons were more generally obtained by the army with the advent of the 'MG 01'. A total of 16 machine gun detachments were formed by 1904. The Model 1901 machine gun was an effective enough weapon, belt fed and water cooled, but massively heavy, and lacked provision for an optical sight. So it was that further development was undertaken, and the MG 08 appeared.

The new machine gun had much in common with its 1901 model predecessor, but was lighter at 18.1 kg for the gun and 34 kg for the *Schlitten* or sledge mount. This mounting was ingenious, and remarkably steady, if unwieldy. For carriage by two or four men it could be folded down like a stretcher – it could also be dragged by means of straps or dismounted so that one or two men could carry the barrel whilst a third put the mount on his back. The *Schlitten* could be adjusted for firing prone or kneeling, and was equipped with pads for the elbows. There was also a box for a small tool kit on the mount to contain lubricants, spare locks, and tongs to remove stuck cartridges. The MG 08 was fitted with flip up iron sights, but had provision for an issue *Zilfernrohr* 12 optical sight. Many guns were also fitted with armoured protection or *Panzerschutz*, the four basic pieces being a water jacket front shield; water jacket top armour; a sledge mount inner shield; and a large armoured shield. This last weighed about 27 kg and made a rather obvious target, and so was usually dispensed with on the Western Front.

Ammunition came in 250 round belts, the usual belt container at the outbreak of war being the *Patronenkaste* Model 1911 which held two belts. Later on, a 1915 model belt box for single belts was introduced, but this was designed so that two boxes could be held back to back in one hand. Given that rapid fire could eat up in excess of a belt a minute, it was usual to keep 16 belts on hand in the gun position and belt store, and a further 12,000 rounds in an immediate reserve. The fabric belts could be filled by means of a small, hand cranked machine or by hand.

In 1914 the standard MG 08 and sledge was employed in both attack and defence, but within a year improvised 'trench mounts' were being introduced with an eye to improved mobility. Almost inevitably such improvisations were less effective for long range sustained fire, though they were handier in the assault. As true 'light' machine guns appeared in the latter part of the war the MG 08 tended to revert to its *Schlitten*. *Regulations for Machine gun Officers and Non-Commissioned Officers*, and an order given to 6th Bavarian Division in 1916, give between them a detailed picture of the duties of a machine gun team in the trenches. Machine gun emplacements were intended to be as unobtrusive as possible, and usually two alternative positions were provided. Only during an engagement was firing to take place from these special positions, any other 'daily firing' being carried

Side view of Erfurt made MG08/15 gun number 767, captured by the 2/5th Battalion the Loyal North Lancashire Regiment at Cambrai, France on 6th October 1918. This weapon has had a chequered history since the Great War, having been in the collection of the Royal West Kents at Maidstone and Bolton Museum before being transferred to the County and Regimental Museum at Preston. Notice the tattered paper webbing strap and, from left to right, the cocking lever, sights and cartridge feed slot.

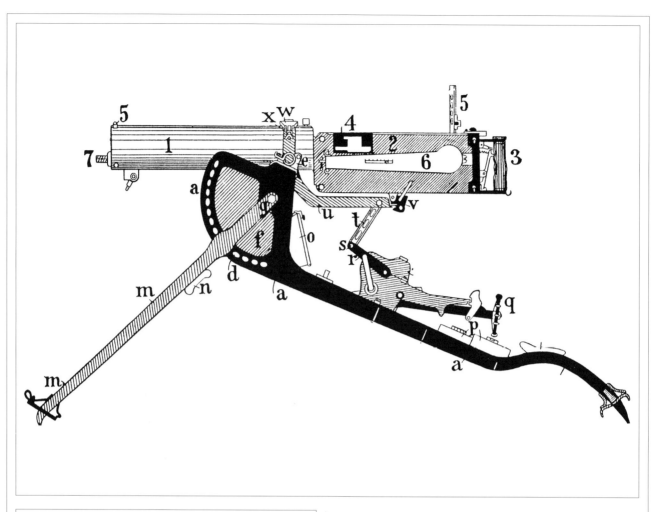

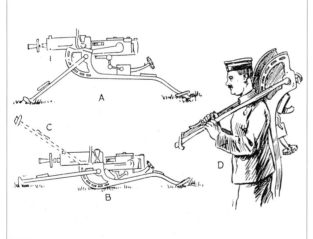

out from elsewhere with pains taken not to damage the wire entanglement. In regular trench systems guns were usually provided with deep dug outs with several exits and brought out only when the bombardment ceased. Since this took time the heavy machine guns were generally only placed in the second or third trench lines. Any spare machine guns were put further back, in clumps of trees or other cover, preferably shielded by wire and covered by infantrymen armed with grenades who could also act as spare gunners.

Any gun crew that ran below 11,500 rounds was expected to report the fact to a Sector Machine Gun Officer who would approach the company commander for more bullets. Other necessaries to be kept near the gun were four spare barrels, a water supply and small-arms for the gun crew including pistols, hand grenades, and a flare pistol. 'Routine' firing was to be conducted in a deliberate manner, checking first that there were no friendly troops to the front, and making use of range cards. In the event of enemy attack, the gun 'Number One' could open fire immediately without regard to such niceties. The Sector Machine Gun Officer and the platoon commander were to be be informed immediately and machine gun regulations and range data destroyed to prevent them falling into enemy hands.

Light Machine Guns

Though the MG 08 proved effective enough it became apparent during the course of 1915 that the Allies were beginning to employ new and deadly automatic weapons which were portable enough to move forward rapidly with attacking troops, giving them a significant tactical advantage. It was very clear that to compete on an even footing there was going to have to be a German light machine gun, issued in quantity. The first step was the appointment of a committee under Colonel Friedrich Von Merkatz, a nobleman who had already been active with the *Gewehr Prufungskommission*, or 'small-arms testing commission'. One option which had definite

Right.

A pintle mounted MG 08 used for railway anti-aircraft defence. The gunners are from more than one unit: the NCO appears to have the railway troops 'E' on his shoulder strap, another man has the number 69. IWM Q 23705.

Below.

A machine gun team with an MG 08 on a light 'trench mount'. The team is directed by an NCO with binoculars and pistol belt; two men fire the gun and the remainder are spare men and ammunition carriers. IWM Q 87923.

Anti-tank action, Western Front, 1918.

Though Germany was slow to develop a tank force of her own she was quick to produce a range of methods aimed at neutralising the effect of Allied armour, including concentrated charges, armour piercing 'K' bullets, individual field guns in the close combat role and finally anti tank rifles. The illustration shows a range of such methods deployed on the 3rd Reserve Division sector of the Western front in 1918. This division faced the French on the Marne during the summer and the British on the Somme during September, taking severe losses. At the end of September it was moved to Belgium.

Right foreground and closely based on a photograph in the Imperial War Museum collection, is a two man anti-tank rifle team drawn from *Füsilier-Regiment Königin Viktoria von Schweden (Pommersches) Nr 34*. The regiment is identifiable by its crowned 'V' monogram on the shoulder straps, though these were sometimes obscured by means of a field grey slide. The men are lightly equipped with gas mask tins, belts and bayonets, the man in the centre of the picture having an all metal *Ersatz* type sidearm and bayonet knot. The 13 mm 'T-Gewehr' anti-tank rifle was essentially an overgrown single shot bolt action Mauser and was introduced in 1918.

The sharpshooter attempting to pick off tank crews or their accompanying infantry, foreground left, is a member of *Reserve-Infanterie Regiment Nr 49*: a unit that Allied intelligence described as 'almost annihilated' in the summer of 1918. He wears the soft *Feldmütze* with grey camouflage strip around the band and carries both a telescope case and a close combat knife on his belt equipment. His weapon is the *Scharfschützen-Gewehr 98* with telescopic sight. Note the variation in the type and colour of the trousers being worn by the men in the foreground.

In the middle distance is a gun of a *Nahkampf* or close combat battery at full recoil. Such guns dealt not only with tanks over open sights, but any sort of breakthrough in their sector. A variety of gun types were in use, of up to 77 mm calibre, but most used special small wheels and were man hauled rather than using animals. On the horizon a British tank is being finished off by a *Flammenwerfer* team. Painting by Christa Hook.

---

attractions was to purchase a gun already under production, but choice was somewhat limited.

A weapon which appeared to have something to recommend it was the Mondragon, perhaps more properly billed as an automatic rifle than a light machine gun. This was a gas-operated, locked breech rifle which had been invented by a Mexican general in the first decade of the century. This worked reasonably well, yet it had at least two significant drawbacks. The first was a susceptibility to malfunction in dirty conditions and the second a drum magazine projecting well below the breech which made prone firing difficult. Reducing the size of the magazine to a small box limited the capacity to only eight rounds. Since in most cases it was intended that the gun would be used by troops lying down in or near filthy trenches, these factors made the Mondragon pretty much a non-starter except as an aircraft weapon, in which capacity it was already serving. Mauser made short recoil automatic rifles similarly received attention. Unfortunately these shared the fault of being too susceptible to dirt, and though they were sometimes fitted with bayonets and full length stocks for infantry use were never widespread.

Another gun which was looked at was the Madsen, a light machine gun originally produced by the Dansk Rekylriffel Syndikat of Copenhagen. This was reliable, weighed just under 10 kg, and had the advantages of a 25 round top loading magazine and a forward bipod. It was also obtained in small numbers by capture from the Russians. These guns were first encountered by the allies in action in the Champagne region in September 1915 and, according to British intelligence, were organised in *Musketen Battalions* of three companies, each of which had 30 guns. The basic unit of deployment was a four man section with a gun, their immediate tactical task being just behind the front line trench, covering any gaps which should occur in the defence. It was believed that the personnel from whom the first of the *Musketen Battalions* was made up had come from the *Grossherzoglich Hessisches*, or Arch Duke of Hesses' Infantry Regiment Nr 117. Though the experiment appears to have been profitable, and Madsen type guns would be seen in German hands for the remainder of the war, the Madsen was no permanent solution to the light machine gun problem.

Small-scale issues were also made of a Theodore Bergmann designed automatic rifle, but again this failed to satisfy demand: it was not terribly reliable, nor available in great quantity. Battle reports continued to complain that the allies, and the British with their Lewis guns in particular, were immeasurably better equipped. In November 1915, Sixth and Third armies noted that 'trench mounts' fitted to the ordinary 08 machine guns served to make them more handy, and that under close assault their relative unsteadiness was not a significant disadvantage. A document submitted by German IV Corps during the battle of the Somme stated that although the *Musketen* or automatic rifles were useful, 'All regiments are unanimous in recommending the introduction of a

Machine gunners of *Ulanen-Regiment von Katzler* unload a captured Russian Model 1910 machine gun from a cart. They all wear lance caps with covers and the *Ulanka* jacket: the man on the left is equipped with machine gun dragging straps. IWM Q 87423.

lighter form of machine gun carriage'.

It seemed that there were only two possible conclusions; either to design a brand new German light machine gun for home manufacture, or to follow the lead of the *Frontschweine* themselves and modify the existing design of a heavy machine gun to make it lighter. Starting afresh would perhaps have been the ideal solution, and there were already interesting avenues of inquiry under investigation including high speed double barrelled guns, and a novel Dreyse machine gun with an unusual locking breech block. Time, however, was of the essence – any new gun would take months to develop and longer still to produce, failure could result in complete catastrophe. The decision was taken to redesign the tried and trusted MG 08, but only in order to reduce weight and improve handling, the basics of the Maxim action would remain unaltered.

The result was the MG 08/15. For a 'light' machine gun it was still a monster, for despite reductions in mass achieved by slimming down the receiver walls, a smaller feed block, a slimmer water jacket, and dispensing with the heavy mount in favour of a handy little bipod, the MG 08/15 still weighed 14 kg empty. A full water jacket and magazine brought the overall weight to 22 kg. Not surprisingly the MG 08/15 was widely regarded as an inferior weapon to the Lewis gun, and would also compare poorly in many respects to the BAR, or Browning Automatic Rifle, which the Americans brought to the war in its closing stages. Nevertheless the MG 08/15 did most of what was wanted and could, if needs be, be carried and fired by one man. It also had the benefit of a 100 round drum magazine, or *trommel* officially known as the *Patronenkasten* 16, which contained the belt, making for more convenient handling and traversing. The bipod was neat, required no setting up, and brought the axis of the gun to about 28 cm over ground level making prone fire highly practical. Though not as stable or accurate as a weapon mounted on a tripod the new machine gun was sighted to 1,900 m. This was doubtless an exaggeration of its realistic capability, but even so it was practical to several hundred metres which was more than adequate for the task in hand.

One sop toward greater portability was the

provision of a webbing and leather sling. In theory this meant that the gun could be fired standing up, with the strap around a shoulder, or even up a tree with the strap around a branch. It is questionable how effective either of these manoeuvres would have been with 22kg of gun, water and ammunition, but nevertheless both these methods of fire continued to feature in post-war manuals. Spare ammunition for the weapon was carried ready loaded in drums, and two drums fitted snugly into a small wooden chest carried by an ammunition gun number when the team was in action.

Production of the new gun was under way in late 1916, but it would be 1917 before any appreciable number were in service at the front, and initially at least many went to the Verdun sector. The majority of the 130,000 guns eventually produced were made in 1918. Though there were seven manufacturers, Spandau made the largest number of MG 08/15s, and this may help to explain why in the English language 'Spandau' came to have common currency to refer to

German machine gunners in the trenches c. 1918 with the 08/15 Light Machine gun. The carrying strap shows, as does a part fired belt. In the trench behind the two man firing team are two gun numbers with ammunition boxes. All the men wear sacking helmet covers and the man on the right has a *Nahkampfmesser* or close combat knife at his belt.

any German light machine gun. In the front line units 'light' MG 08/15 weapons would finally outnumber the 'heavy' MG 08 by four to one, whilst in the army as a whole the proportion was more like five to two. Even artillery batteries were issued with a few for close quarters defence.

By March 1917, the approved scale of issue was three guns per infantry company throughout the army, a figure which was later raised to six guns per company, or two for every platoon. At first the guns were kept in a separate fourth 'support' platoon, but eventually as numbers allowed the light machine guns were parcelled out to the platoons, so that each platoon now had a light machine gun squad. Ultimately, in the final days of the war, there were even *Einheits-Gruppe*, fully integrated squads which included a light machine gun, and the MG 08/15 became the universal support weapon. It was intended to be rushed forward with the attack in order to support the riflemen or deal with strong points, and in the defence it was to add flexibility, economising on front line troops.

Just how effective this could be was made plain to men of 2nd Battalion Royal Welch Fusiliers, during an advance made near Le Transloy on 1 September 1918: 'We could not say what had happened, but we came suddenly face to face with an inferno of machine gun

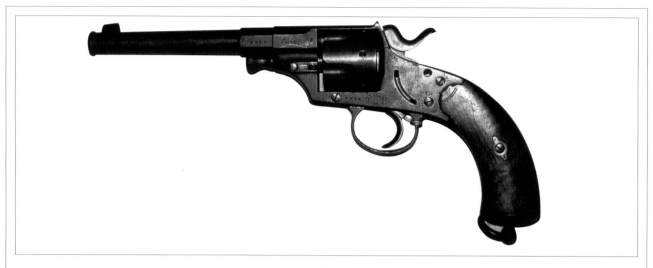

The obsolete Model 1879 Reichs revolver which was still issued to artillery drivers and certain reservists in 1914. SB.

fire while we were yet in very open country. There was a general scattering of the two leading companies, and we took cover wherever we could. I dropped into a shell hole in the middle of an open field, and the other signallers near me did likewise ... C Company was suddenly met with an appalling and withering burst of machinegun and rifle fire from the front and left front – the west and north west of Sailly-Saillisel. Our fellows went down like nine pins, and soon all was confusion ... He got 20 yards, and went down with a shot through his head. Our only hope was to get on, to stay was to be slaughtered. I shouted to the men to rush the railway, and started towards it myself. I got perhaps 50 yards, when I crumpled up with a bullet through the leg which split the tendon'. Not long after the Germans launched a text-book counter attack, pushing their support weapons up with them, and taking advantage of local success to place their machineguns within 400 yards of the main position, 'They then settled down without delay to get their light machine guns to work'. It had been a classic

example of *Flachen und Lucken*, a patch work of 'defended areas' and swept 'gaps' into which the enemy had pressed, and exposed themselves to retaliation. The situation was only stabilised by the British use of Lewis guns, and the timely intervention of a couple of extra companies of the South Wales Borderers.

There was no doubt that the MG 08/15 did its job, providing a machine weapon that was capable of giving squad support, which also could be manufactured in quantity, and required comparatively little retraining for those accustomed to the MG 08. Its advantages included a 100 round magazine capacity, the use of the standard rifle cartridge and a good sustained fire capability. On the other hand the MG 08/15 was undoubtedly one of the heaviest 'light' machineguns ever made, and even Ludendorff complained in his *War Memoirs* that the gun should have been both lighter and smaller. In terms of manageability it would never quite match the Lewis gun which it was intended to combat.

Pistols and Sub MachineGuns

In theory the standard issue pistol of the German army was the Model 1908 semi automatic. Despite being universally known as the *Luger* pistol, Georg

The Mauser C96 *Broomhandle* semi-automatic pistol; one of many types pressed into service during the war.

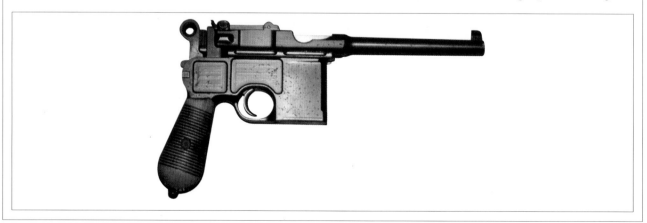

The wooden holster for the Mauser C96 which also doubled as a shoulder stock.

Luger (1849 – 1923) was just one of several designers whose work contributed to the appearance of this remarkable weapon. The 'toggle' lock mechanism, for example, was first successfully applied to firearms by Hiram Stevens Maxim, and had been refined for use in a semi automatic pistol by Hugo Borchardt of Magdeburg. Tests at Enfield showed that the Luger was a weapon of outstanding potential, being: 'well made. . . of good design, and handles comfortably. . . an important advantage that this pistol possesses is the fact, when the eight rounds have been fired, that the magazine can be replaced by a full one and fire resumed in four or five seconds.' Furthermore, it was found to have good penetration, its bullet being capable of passing through at least 14 half-inch deal boards, and it was relatively straightforward to strip and clean.

In German trials, the Luger found itself in competition with a number of other designs, most notably the Mauser C96, now commonly known as the 'Broomhandle' Mauser, itself an innovative early semi automatic. By 1904, the Luger had proved itself superior in almost every respect, including reliability,

The standard issue single shot flare pistol.

and given a few further modifications the decision was taken to equip German forces with the new pistol. First came the Imperial German Navy which, having conducted brief tests of its own at Kiel, ordered its first significant numbers of the 9 mm *Selbstlade-Pistolen Modell* 1904 (or self loading model 1904 pistol), with a 15 cm barrel, in the latter part of that year.

The Luger first saw action in German East Africa and South West Africa in 1905. Perhaps surprisingly the soldiery were not overly impressed, and rifles were preferred in almost every circumstance. Clearly the new pistols were not that well cared for since several had suffered minor breakages and some had gone rusty. This was perhaps an indicator of the weapons future Achilles heel: it was a remarkable pistol, accurate, well engineered and superbly designed, but without care and respect it was more prone to malfunction than a comparatively less sophisticated revolver.

Issues were made to experimental machinegun detachments in 1907 and orders for the adoption of the Luger pistol were signed by Kaiser Wilhelm II on 22 August 1908, hence the *Pistole 08* designation of the standard army model. The first major contract for the P 08 was 50,000 weapons from the *Deutsche Waffen und Munitionsfabriken*, or *DWM* in November that year. Despite being essentially similar to the P 04

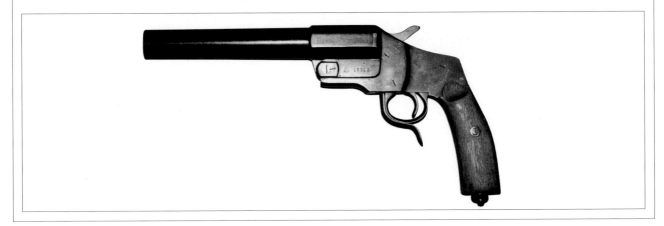

naval pistol the new army weapon did have significant differences. Perhaps most obviously the army model had a shorter 10 cm barrel, but it also lacked the 'grip safety' which had characterised the early examples of the 'P 04'. Instead the army model had only a simple manual lever which acted directly on the sear bar.

By 1910 production for the German army was in full swing, and DWM had been joined in manufacture by Erfurt, the Prussian government arms factory. To go with the new weapon a standard model holster was approved, officially called the *Pistolen Tasche 1908*, or 'P.T. 08'. This was made of stiff leather and fully enclosed the gun, having a flap top secured by a strap.

Left.

A Saxon infantryman throwing stick grenades, 1915. The handles of the bombs are of the early type with rounded ends; only one set of ammunition carriers are worn by the soldier allowing two grenades to be suspended by their hooks on the other side of the belt. SB.

Below.

Assault troops from a variety of units in a shell hole with several different grenades and a messenger dog which carries bombs in a miniature vest. The men are lightly equipped; one has two water bottles, another a greatcoat or shelter sheet rolled around his shoulder.

Top.

An officer with the G 98 rifle, grenade launching stand and Model 1914 rifle grenade. SB.

Right.

Men of Grenadier Regiment Nr 12 or Reserve Infantry Regiment Nr 12 preparing to fire Model 1914 rifle grenades. Notice the use of the lanyard to set off the rifle and the box of grenade heads in the foreground. IWM Q 23932.

It also featured a compartment for a spare magazine and internal stowage for a stripping tool. Later conversions were also made from old 1891 model revolver holsters. By the end of 1910 machine gunners and infantry specialists in the standing army had received their new pistols, with cavalry distribution commencing thereafter and finishing in 1911. Last to be issued were men of the artillery and airship crews. Officers' pistols, when privately purchased, cost 47.50 Marks.

As early as 1913 a special *Lange*, or long barrelled version of the Luger pistol was approved for the field artillery and airmen. An order for over 200,000 such arms was made in 1914, though the majority of the examples of this 20 cm barrel variant seen by the present writer have been dated 1917 and 1918. The

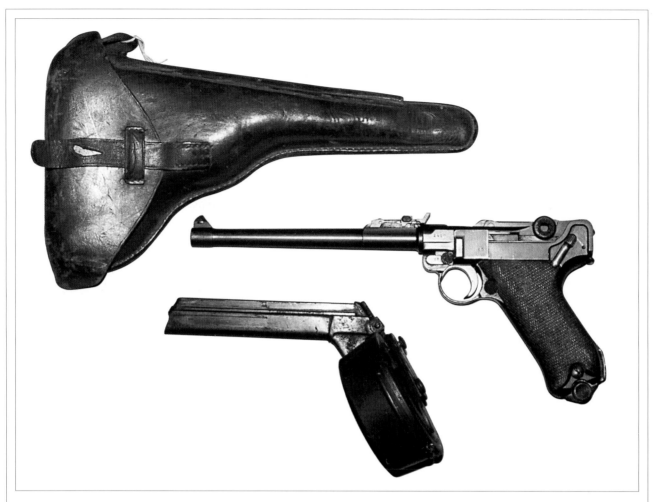

The Luger *Lange* pistol which was issued to the artillery and, with the aid of a wooden shoulder stock and drum magazine, could be used as a species of carbine.

Lange pistol was issued with a flat board type detachable shoulder stock, and was often used in conjunction with a 32 round drum or 'snail' magazine, known as the *Trommelmagazin*. The first known patent for such a device was that taken out by the Hungarians Tatarek and von Benko in 1911, but a further improvement was filed by Friedrich Blum of Budapest in 1915. The *Lange* Pistole was sighted to a remarkably optimistic 800 metres, its manual claiming effectiveness at a head-sized target up to 600 metres and an ability to penetrate the French steel helmet at 800 metres.

Though the *Lange* Pistole was undoubtedly handier than a carbine, and was semi-automatic, it is dubious that anything like this performance could be expected under battle conditions. Recent tests have shown that under ideal circumstances a stationary, man-sized target in the open at 400 metres, can be very difficult to hit. It therefore seems reasonable to suppose that in action, against partial fleeting targets, a practical range of perhaps 200 metres was more realistic. Nevertheless it is interesting that this

weapon, and experiments with fully automatic Luger carbines, did help illustrate the need for a relatively short range, light, automatic or semi automatic weapon for trench use which was more effective than an ordinary pistol. About 1.6 million Luger pistols of all types were made by the end of the Great War, and they earned the affection of the troops. They fired rapidly, pointed easily and were superb pistols for their time, giving excellent service if properly cared for.

Though the needs of the pre-war regular army for Luger pistols were pretty well satisfied by 1914 when hostilities commenced, the expansion of the army rapidly outstripped industrial capacity. The result was that particularly in rear echelon formations, 'train' units, the *Landsturm*, and the like, other pistols and obsolete revolvers were pressed into service. These other patterns, generally known as *Behelfspistolen*, included not only significant numbers of the Mauser C96 in 9 mm, but Behollas, Dreyses, Bayards and even Belgian-made Brownings, some of these were in 7.65 mm, some even in 6.35 mm. The Bavarians imported at least small numbers of the Austrian Steyr-Hahn *Repetierpistolen* M12.

It was only in mid-1918 that a more effective close assault weapon reached the troops in the form of the Bergmann 9 mm 'machine pistol', the first effective

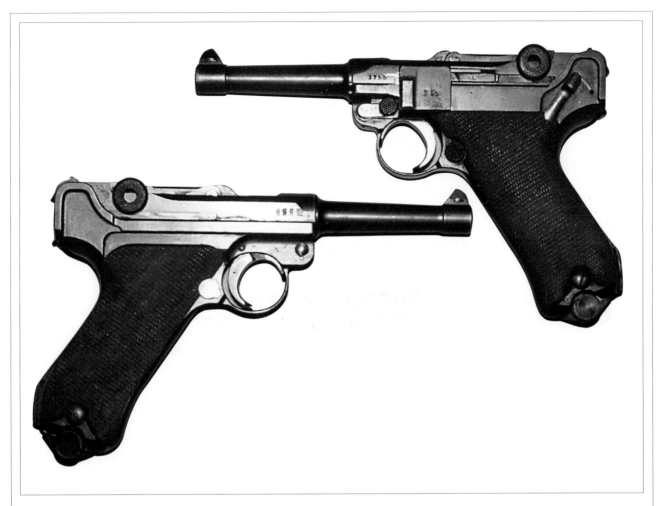

sub-machine gun. As its German nomenclature suggested, the Bergmann owed quite a debt to pistol technology, firing the standard military pistol round, and using the same 32 round drum magazine which was fitted to the *Lange* pistole. It was issued to officers, NCOs and ten men in each assault company and sometimes to small squads within other units, but it is thought that no more than 30,000 were produced by the end of hostilities. Thus it was that a revolutionary new weapon had only a limited impact on the war.

Grenades

Grenades, which were relatively unimportant throughout much of the 19th century, sprang suddenly to prominence with the trench stalemate of the Great War. Though supplies were limited at the outbreak,

Germany had three major types: a time fused hand-grenade; a percussion hand-grenade; and a rodded rifle grenade. The time fused hand grenade, known as the *Kügelhandgranate*, or 'ball hand grenade', Model 1913, was a cast iron sphere segmented on the outside and fitted with a brass fuze. A pull on the wire loop, often assisted by means of a hook, ignited the fuze, and after seven seconds the main black powder charge was ignited. The *Kügelhandgranate* was a relatively low technology weapon, but was well suited to use from cover where the thrower was himself protected from the fragments. A slightly simplified version was introduced as the Model 1915. The *Diskushandgranate* Model 1913 was a percussion, or explode on impact model bomb. This comprised an oyster-like iron shell with six projections around the edge. Once the safety pin had been removed the bomb could be thrown and impact caused a striker to ignite the detonator which in turn exploded the main charge. Though not totally reliable this was thought useful enough for a new type to be produced in 1915, which was slightly larger and had a thin steel outer shell.

The rodded rifle grenades were of two main types, models 1913 and 1914. These weighed about 1 kg, and though they differed in detail in both instances the method of discharge was similar. The rod of the

bomb was slid down the barrel of the rifle and any safety disengaged: next the rifle was loaded with a blank cartridge, and when the rifle was fired the bomb was launched to explode on impact. In the 1913 version ranging discs could be added to the nose of the bomb, in the 1914 type the ranging discs were added to the base. Rifle grenades could be used in conjunction with a launching stand, the issue version of which was a substantial equipment with carrying handles, an elevating arc, and a large spring to absorb the recoil of the rifle.

By the end of 1914 it was apparent that the demand for grenades of all types was far outstripping supply. The result was that like their enemies the German armies resorted to all manner of

Left.

A selection of grenade types displayed in a trench, 1915. Between the two stick grenades are two tins with friction igniters; a Model 1913 Discus bomb and a Model 1913 *Kügel* hand grenade. SB.

Below.

Two different ways of using the basic stick grenade: as part of a Bangalore torpedo for blowing wire and other obstructions, or in a 'concentrated charge', useful against bunkers and tanks.

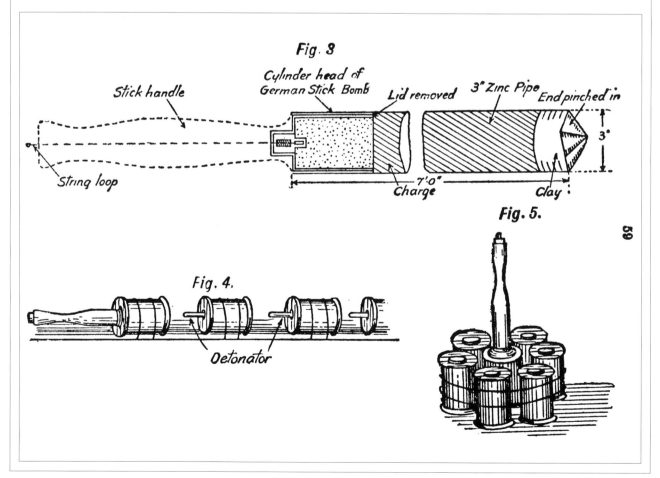

The new 7.6 cm light *Minenwerfer*, August 1917. The usual fighting detachment was a 'Trupp' of a couple of NCOs and four or five crewmen. The infantry group shown here includes an NCO distinguished by his peaked cap and collar braid and a signaller with field telephone. Ankle boots and puttees are in evidence: some men wear the *Bluse* and grey strips are worn over some of the cap bands obscuring the lower cap cockade. The mortar is loaded from the muzzle and fired by means of a pull on the lanyard. SB.

Right.

The rifle grenade launching stand with its huge recoil absorbing springs and elevating device.

improvisations and emergency models. Some of these, including explosives crammed into tin cans, or strapped to racquet-style handles were actually manufactured in the field. Others, incorporating simple spring igniters, or fuses like overgrown match heads, were made in the home factories.

It was in 1915 that the best known of the German grenades actually appeared. This *Stielhandgranate* or stick grenade was soon to become a standard, though in fact there were several slightly different versions of the basic concept. By far the commonest was the

Stielhandgranate 'B.Z.', which British intelligence described accurately enough as the 'Cylindrical hand grenade, with handle and time fuse, regulation type'. The main components of this were a cylindrical steel head containing the explosive, a wooden handle, a friction igniter, and a detonator. The head was stencilled with the legend, *Vor Gebrauch Sprengkapsel Einsetzen*, meaning 'before use insert the detonator'. To use the grenade the soldier first untaped the pull cord from the base of the handle, then gave the cord a smart pull which activated the friction igniter. The fuse thus lit, there were five and a half seconds before

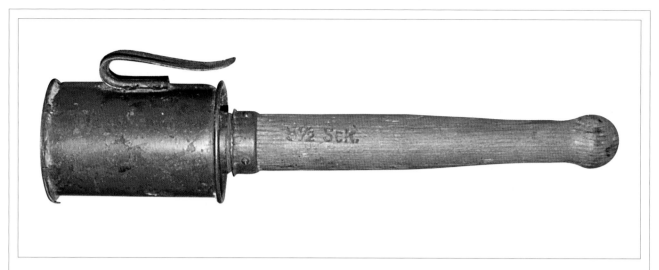

the detonator went off exploding the main charge. By about 1916 there were alterations to the handle and cord arrangement so that now the cord was concealed underneath a screw cap, and the cord terminated in a porcelain button. These modifications made the ignition system less susceptible to damp, and had the added advantage of giving something more substantial to grasp when lighting the grenade. There were also less common versions of the stick grenade including the *Wilhelm's Handgranate A.Z.* which was an explode on impact type, and a model which used a spring igniter. All of the stick bombs were regarded as principally offensive bombs, working more by blast effect than by fragmentation. They were thus more localised in their impact, and better suited to troops crossing open terrain.

The year 1916 also saw the introduction of a new time fuse hand grenade, the *Eierhandgranate*, or 'egg grenade', a relatively small, iron ovoid full of explosive which was lit by a pull fuse. This was designed essentially with range in mind, and was intended to be of sufficient power to clear a single bay of a trench. In the assault, troops armed with egg bombs were to work in close co-operation with stick bomb throwers. The stick bombers would engage at close to medium ranges, whilst the egg bomb throwers would aim at the furthest targets, thus impeding enemy reinforcement and the passing forward of supplies of bombs during grenade duels.

Rodded rifle grenade production was phased out during 1916, and in 1917 a replacement was introduced in the form of the *Wurf* grenade. This little grenade, characterised by the Allies as a 'jam pot bomb' was also a rifle grenade but, unlike the rodded types, was launched from a discharger cup fitted to the end of the rifle. Alarmingly enough it was projected by means of a bulleted round. When the bullet was fired it passed up through a channel in the middle of the bomb, which both ignited the fuse and provided sufficient gas to propel the bomb into the air. It was thus essentially similar to the French 'V.B.' system.

The use of grenades, as mentioned above, was an integral part of the evolution of small unit tactics. Thus it was that the first *Stoss* or shock troops of the war were mere handfuls of men, often drawn from the ordinary infantry units and armed not only with bombs but improvised shields, clubs, knives and sharpened entrenching tools for close quarter work against limited objectives. By 1915 the idea of a *Handgranatentrupp* of six to eight men was current, the members of the group being selected according to their skill with the bomb and their personal courage. These troops were later often marked out by special insignia, sometimes in the form of a crude stick grenade shape worn on the upper arm, and were trained in both offensive and defensive grenade tactics.

Detailed instructions to the members of the

Handgrenatentrupp of third battalion Reserve Infantry Regiment Nr 235 in December 1915 specified that when responding to an enemy incursion into the trench line they would equip themselves so that: 'All men of the party carry their rifles slung, bayonets fixed and daggers ready, with the exception of the two leaders, who do not carry rifles. The latter may carry as many grenades as they can conveniently handle and should, if possible, be armed with pistols. The commander, similarly armed, follows the two leading men. If no pistols are available the commander, carries his rifle ready loaded in his hands. The remaining three men follow the others one traverse to the rear; they keep within sight of their commander and carry as many grenades as possible.' The group thus constituted would work its way along the trenches, the lead men crouching and the commander firing over them as necessary. The enemy would be tracked down and outfought, intervals between traverses being taken at the rush. Where a natural break occurred or where it was thought best to attempt to contain the enemy, 'trench blocks' or breast works would be erected across the trench.

Such methods were further refined with time so that by later in 1916 *Gruppe* of nine men were deployed including two subsections of four under a squad leader. The front subsection included two throwers and two close support carriers who were also armed with knives and pistols, but when need arose all four would shower the enemy with bombs simultaneously. The rear subsection went armed with rifles and bayonets but also carried more bombs and empty sand bags secured by their haversack straps. The whole *Gruppe* would advance well spread out so as to minimise the effects of enemy retaliation. They would bomb over traverses systematically, the group number two shouting '*Geraümt!*', or 'cleared!', as each obstacle was secured, allowing the leader to order the resumption of the advance. Cleared areas could be marked with small flags, and when it was required to secure a sector the order '*Sandsäche Vor* ', or '*sandbags to the front !*', was given. A blockade was then built between the two subsections, the front four men retiring across it when completed. Finally grenade squads would themselves be integrated into the all arms *Sturmabteilung*, and *Sturmkompanien* which were such a feature of German offensive action later in the war.

Artillery

Like most European nations the German artillery arm made significant advances in the three decades prior to

'Help us Win!': the very famous picture by Professor Fritz Erler of Munich which appeared as both a postcard and a poster in support of the War Loans campaign in 1917. The figure depicted is an assault infantryman of a senior regiment, carrying both gas mask and bag of stick grenades. Note how the grenades have had their safety caps removed allowing the cords to dangle free, ready for use at a moment's notice.(SB)

the war. After 1914 it not only developed progressively in range and quantity, but in terms of quality, with improved shells, better communications and vastly improved tactics. Operations now concentrated on long range predicted fire; whirlwind bombardments; creeping barrages known graphically in German as *Feuerwalzen*; denial of parts of the battlefield; and counter battery fire. Proportionately fewer of the available guns were committed to the battlefield firing over open sights, but there were deployments of close range batteries both as a means to support attacks and as a backstop against enemy advances. Artillery finally became both the vital tool to reopen fluid action and the prime slayer of Allied personnel. A single artillery unit, *Feld-Artillerie-Regiment* Nr 79, was able to report that after 1,181 days of war it had fired 667,100 rounds, more than the total fired in the Franco–Prussian War.

A 21 cm *Mörser* of the foot artillery with its ammunition and crew. Notice that the gun wheels are equipped with special steel and wooden shoes for muddy terrain and that the huge shells are protected by wicker cases prior to use. Many of the crew are in shirt sleeves and caps for heavy labour; one man is wearing a cardigan.

Even by 1913 the Field Artillery establishment was 642 batteries, and the majority of the weapons were modern 'Quick Firers' with integral recoil mechanisms, using fixed charges of ammunition. The basic field gun was the 77 mm *Feldkanone* 96, which had first been introduced in 1896, and was modified in 1905 and 1906. The 77 mm was shielded, and had a range of about 9,000 m. It was towed into action behind a limber which carried an immediate supply of 36 shells. An updated version of the gun with an improved carriage appeared in 1916, this becoming known as the *Feldkanone* 16, or FK 16. The main model of field howitzer was the 10.5 cm *Feldhaubitze* 98 / 09, introduced in 1898 and modified in 1909. This was also shielded, and had a range of approximately 7,000 m. This howitzer was similarly improved during the war, with the models 'IFH 16' and 'IFH Kp' having improved carriages and ranges in excess of 9,000 m.

Heavier weapons were the province of the Foot Artillery. The commonest heavy howitzer was the 15 cm *Schwere Feldhaubitze*, several different models of which were in existence by the outbreak of war with varying types of carriage and maximum ranges of between 6,000 and 8,500 yards. Larger again in scale was the 21 cm, and though the technical nomenclature for this weapon was the 21 cm *Mörser*, this was mounted on a carriage much like any other heavy howitzer. Other than these guns the Foot Artillery also manned a wide variety of weapons of between 9 cm and 42 cm calibre, ranging from obsolete and captured heavy pieces through to the monster fortress busters since dubbed 'Big Berthas'. Perhaps the most extraordinary gun of all was the modified version of the 38 cm 'Long Max', a supercharged long range gun operating in the latter part of the war, which was capable of blasting its shells into the stratosphere, and reaching Paris from behind the German lines. More than half a century later this would be the inspiration for the Iraqi 'super gun'.

Trench Mortars

As soon as the Western Front became deadlocked with trenches and shell holes, the value of weapons which

Men of a *Landwehr* battery with a 10.5 cm light field howitzer (*Leichte Feldhaubitze 98 / 09*) on an anti-aircraft mounting.

could lob large projectiles at high angles into the enemy lines was recognised. Though some mortars were accepted as early as 1910, at the outbreak of war the German army could boast only 70 heavy, and 116 medium weapons. As might be expected the result was a massive drive to produce more equipments. Many of these were improvised by the troops themselves, some from gas pipes, others from tubes sunk into the ground and known as 'earth mortars'. As the Commanding Officer of Army Group Fleck reported in his secret memorandum 756, of July 1915: 'The employment of the *Minenwerfer* has developed during the course of the present war, and in a very remarkable way. At the beginning of trench warfare, we only had at our disposal a small number of *Minenwerfer*, and neither the higher nor the subordinate commanders in our infantry possessed any definite ideas as to their employment. The French, who at first were absolutely unprovided with *Minenwerfer*, naturally suffered severely from the destructive effects of these weapons; they began by extemporising them, since they have never ceased in their efforts to perfect them and their output has increased up to the present moment. After

some time they were able to concentrate a large number of *Minenwerfer* and gained superiority of fire. Gradually however, we have overtaken the French, both as regards numbers and the proper use of these weapons. Nevertheless, their tactical employment in many respects leaves much to be desired...'

One of the weapons which helped to gain the upper hand was the 17 cm medium trench mortar. This stubby beast had come into being as a result of experiments conducted prior to the war by the Prussian engineer corps which suggested that a bomb weight of 50 kg was necessary against barbed wire and screens, and that an accurate range of over 300 metres was needed. If anything the 17 cm *Mittlerer Minenwerfer* was almost too elaborate for the task in hand. It was a rifled muzzle loader with a sturdy base, elevating and traversing wheels and very accurate, but the huge solid barrel and luxurious mount with sprung recoil buffers were immensely heavy at 483 kg. Another drawback was that on the original mount traverse was limited to 25 degrees. Rather than abandon the design altogether it was decided to change the platform, this leading to the introduction of a new circular mount, even heavier than the first, and this saw service in the latter part of the war. Transporting such a mass of machinery caused

One way to sound the gas alarm in 1917: with a frying pan and stick. Note the gas mask slung around the neck. IWM 55224.

model of the 7.6 cm was introduced in 1916, and was capable of throwing up to 20 high explosive or gas shells per minute to a range of 1,300 metres. Though not technically mortars, *Granatenwerfer* were also used from the middle of the war. These threw a 2 kg bomb approximately 300 metres, and by 1918 were issued on a scale of four per battalion.

There were several tactical techniques which could be used to improve the effectiveness of 'Minnie' fire. In counter battery, for example, it was usual to concentrate the medium *Minenwerfer* backed with conventional artillery prior to the shoot. Then just a handful of the mortars would commence firing. When the enemy replied his positions were pinpointed and the German task force would shoot in overwhelming strength. Against trench lines it soon became apparent that an alert enemy would either vacate a section of trench, or take to deep cover when under mortar fire. The obvious counter-measures were erratic shoots; a barrage laid first on the section of trench to be attacked and then a few yards behind, and infantry assaults the moment 'Minnie' fire ceased.

According to German army organisation of late 1915 each division had attached two heavy (25 cm), four medium and six light trench mortars. During the next year exponential increases allowed the transfer of four light trench mortars to every infantry battalion, whilst the divisional artillery mortar companies maintained an establishment of four heavy and eight medium weapons. In 1918 the heavier weapons were also turned over to the infantry. In January of that year there were 1,322 heavy, 2,476 medium and 13, 329 light trench mortars in service.

Gas and Gas Masks

Though there had been experiments elsewhere gas was first introduced to the Western Front by the German army in the spring of 1915, initially by means of cylinder release, with devastating effect. Very quickly, however, the Allies realised that given adequate protection and some warning, gas was not necessarily a lethal wonder weapon, and they began to respond in kind. Later German efforts were concentrated both on the development of new types of gas and on its delivery by shell from artillery and mortars. Eventually, like the British, the Germans were using specialised gas projectors or *Gaswerfer* in massed batteries. Early poison gases like chlorine and phosgene were supplemented by more virulent agents such as mustard gas which burned the skin. Gas shells were distinguished by a series of coloured crosses to denote their content, as for example Green Cross,

problems. Road movement was not too bad since the medium trench mortar came with its own pair of wheels which allowed it to be horse drawn, or in case of extremis, pulled by the crew. Movement across the trenchscape was another matter: for the final journey to the emplacement there was usually nothing for it but dismantling, and the use of no less than 17 men as porters. Four of these were required to carry the barrel alone.

Despite the efforts involved the 17 cm mortar was an extremely valuable weapon, as was suggested in the instructions issued on the use of *Minenwerfer*: 'The medium *Minenwerfer* is specially employed by the defence in siege warfare, against the attacker's works, sap heads, bomb proofs (for instance, immediately prior to an attack), and also to hamper the enemy's movements in his communication trenches. In the attack, also, it is used for the destruction of obstacles and against houses and the edges of woods and villages. Its splinters are also very effective against animate targets'.

At the smaller end of the scale, 7.6 cm trench mortars were also soon deployed. The 'new' light which was diphosgene, or Yellow Cross which was mustard gas.

From the start of gas warfare, the German Army made some use of crude impregnated pads as protection, though these were of limited effectiveness. Indeed the official advice to men so equipped was to 'breathe as little and as calmly as possible'. It was not long before concerted effort produced a gas mask which was both handy and practical, the basics of which would last the war. The new mask was essentially of two elements; a rubberised cloth face piece with two circular windows for the eyes, and the filter cylinder containing a granular powder which was attached to the face piece by means of screw thread metal fittings. A long tape allowed the mask to be hung around the neck, and shorter elasticated bands were used to hold it to the face. The face piece was in three sizes '1' which was large, '2' which was medium and '3' which was small.

Where possible the various components of the equipment had been designed so that they could be made on types of machinery that were already available, thus it was that the screw fitting joining mask and filter was of the same dimensions as those utilised in Osram street lamps, and the production facility for one could be switched fairly quickly to make the other. The first design of carry case was a soft, grey cloth bag capable of taking a complete mask and a spare filter, closed by a single button and attached to the soldiers' belt by means of two loops. In the field, bags were sometimes modified by the addition of metal rings which allowed the cloth bag to be suspended on a haversack sling. Manufacture of the new mask system commenced in September 1915.

The combination of face piece and cylinder linked directly together had both advantages and disadvantages. Amongst the benefits were the fact that the arrangement required no clumsy pipes or bags; that the whole thing only used about 20 components, and that when the filter required changing it was a simple task to unscrew one and fit another. It was also useful that when the filter specification was up rated it was not necessary to discard the whole system, but simply to design new filter types to fit the existing face piece. On the downside it was true that the filter effectively hung from the face, and that if the mask was not to become unduly unwieldy filters would have to be kept reasonably compact. So it was that the German mask filter had a much more limited cubic capacity than the Anglo-American Small Box Respirators and was marginally less effective than the Allied design, and only good for rather shorter periods.

An artillery driver and his team protected against gas. The primitive bags over the muzzles of the horses were inefficient, but did at least prevent the eating of contaminated fodder. IWM Q 55085.

Apart from the introduction of improved filters there were two major changes which would alter significantly the outward appearance of the gas mask between 1915 and the end of the war. The first, and most obvious, was the introduction of a tin stowage cylinder, intended to replace the less resilient cloth bag. The field grey painted tin, introduced in 1916, was usually carried by means of a shoulder strap,although it could be hung from the belt. Shoulder straps of various types are seen but one particularly common later in the war was made of woven paper, so saving on leather and other materials. When issued the tin contained an instruction sheet in the bottom of the can, and spare mask lenses in a compartment in the lid. The tin case was effective enough but in circumstances where quiet was important the cloth bag was preferred.

The second major change to the gas mask was entirely driven by the shortage of rubberised fabric which by 1917 had become critical. So it was that during that year a new pattern face mask was

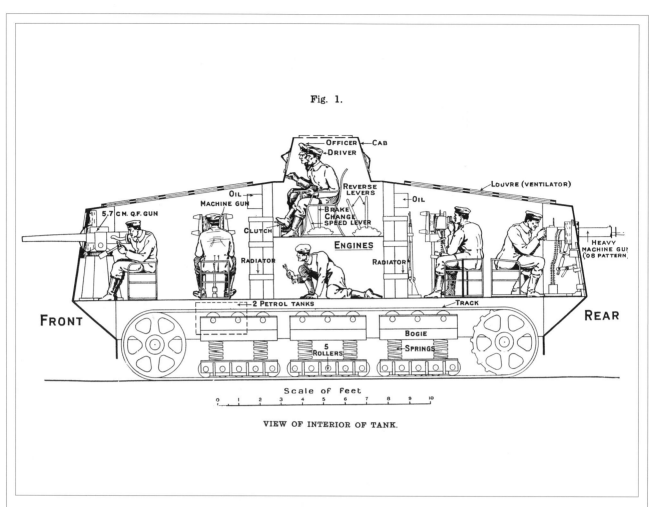

Fig. 1.

VIEW OF INTERIOR OF TANK.

The interior of the A7V as depicted in a British intelligence report. Very few of these tanks saw service in 1918.

introduced which dispensed with the need for rubber altogether. Amazingly, the main constituent of the new face piece was Bulgarian, chrome tanned, sheep leather. This was dipped into a sealing oil to render it waterproof, then cut so that it could be rolled into a cone shape and the seams stitched and lacquered. The eye pieces were double layered and coated internally, in an attempt to prevent misting. Since the leather was less flexible than the old fabric it was not possible to incorporate the little cleaning folds by means of which the soldier had been able to wipe the lenses of the old mask without removal. The mask also required the incorporation of a system of wires to hold it firmly against the face. Ingenious though the new Model 1917 'sheep leather' mask undoubtedly was, it was in many small ways inferior to the original. It smelt, was more difficult to fit, was more problematic in the rain, and tended to assume a different geometry to the old mask whereby the eyepieces were at an angle to the eye. Shooting was therefore more difficult than in the rubberised fabric mask. By mid 1918 leather masks were overtaking the old style masks numerically, but both continued through to the Armistice.

One other breathing equipment in use was the Draeger Oxygen Apparatus, though this elaborate system complete with its own oxygen cylinder was intended primarily as a 'breathing set' for use by tunnellers and machinegunners in inadequately ventilated emplacements. Each pioneer company was intended to be supplied with 25 sets; each machinegun company with six; and each infantry company with three. Every Draeger *Selbstretter* set was to be accompanied by a nose clip and three pairs of anti-gas goggles.

According to German instructions issued in July 1916 a senior special officer was attached to every army with responsibility for gas defence. This *GasSchutzoffizier* had amongst other things to organise gas mask training, inspection of appliances and the collection of information which was to be communicated to the relevant department of the War Ministry. His task was aided by more junior officers at both Corps and Divisional level who, amongst other things, would ensure that the correct levels of equipment were maintained. This provision was intended to be one ordinary mask per man in every unit within four kilometres of the front, plus a unit reserve of 10%. Each mask was to have two filters, with a further two filters per mask in various reserve stores.

Sample Divisions and Establishments

The following selection of 20 sample divisions, from various battles and fronts, has been abstracted from Histories of the *Two Hundred and Fifty-One Divisions of the German Army Which Participated in the War*, 1914–1918 compiled by the intelligence section of the American General Staff at Chaumont, France, in 1919. For the sake of clarity and brevity only infantry, cavalry and artillery units have been included in the examples; engineers and other supporting arms have been omitted.

At the start of the war it was usual for an Army Corps to be made up of two divisions plus a *Jäger* battalion, a pioneer battalion, four batteries of heavy artillery, a bridging train, signals units, supply columns, field hospitals and field bakeries. The total strength of a 1914 Army Corps was thus about 44,000 men. The infantry divisions themselves were each composed of two brigades, each brigade of two regiments, giving 12 battalions per division supported by 72 guns.

Very quickly it became necessary both to make manpower savings and to create more flexible units. From March 1915 on the instigation of Colonel Ernst von Wrisberg of the Prussian War Ministry, divisions began to be produced with only one infantry brigade of three regiments. These nine battalion divisions had just one artillery regiment of 36 guns and totalled about 12,500 men. Nevertheless it was some time before this organisation became the norm. It was also noticeable that there was a distinct hierarchy amongst the various types of division, so that the best were frequently employed as 'shock' or attack divisions. The less effective formations, like the *Landwehr*, and the dismounted cavalry divisions of the latter part of the war, tended to be used as defensive or holding units. Many of these less effective divisions were used to maintain the vast sectors of the quieter parts of the Eastern Front.

1st Guard Division: Flanders and the Marne, 1914

1st Guard Brigade: 1. *Garde zu Fuß*; 3. *Garde zu Fuß*
2nd Guard Brigade: 2. *Garde zu Fuß*; 4. *Garde zu Fuß*
1st Guard Artillery
Brigade: *Garde* artillery regiments 1 and 3.

The 1st Guard Division entered Belgium on 13 August 1914 and was engaged at Fosse, St Gerard, Fournaux and Le Sourd. In September it was on the Marne facing Foch's Ninth French Army in the St Gond marshes sector. At least part of the division was at Gheluvelt in Flanders, and by early 1915 the 3 *Garde zu Fuß* alone had taken almost 3,000 casualties, its approximate pre-war strength. Nevertheless American intelligence would continue to consider the 1st Guard Division 'one of the very best German shock divisions'.

54th Reserve Division: Ypres 1914

107th Reserve Brigade: 245 and 246
                          Reserve Regiments
108th Reserve Brigade: 247 and 248
                          Reserve Regiments
                          26 Reserve Jäger Battalion
                          54 Reserve Cavalry
                          Detachment
54 Reserve Field Artillery
Regt.   (nine batteries 1–3 Saxon,
                          4–9 Württemburg)

The 54th Reserve Division was mainly from Württemburg with the addition of some Saxon troops. It first saw action in Belgium in October 1914; it took part in the attack on Gheluvelt, and was at Zonnebeke in the general attack of 11 November. In a single month 248 Reserve Regiment alone lost more than 1,400 officers and men.

3rd Reserve Division: Tannenberg, 1914

5th Reserve Brigade: 2 and 9 Reserve Regiments
6th Reserve Brigade: 34 and 49 Reserve Regiments
                     5. Reserve Dragoon Regiment
                     (3 squadrons)
                     3 Reserve Artillery Regiment
                     (six batteries)

3rd Reserve Division was recruited in Pomerania and was a part of the German Eighth Army under Hindenburg. It was engaged at the successful battle of Tannenberg against the Russians in August 1914, and subsequently in action at Biallo, Lyck, Suwalki and Augustowo during the following two months. In early 1915, and without substantial change to the order of battle, it fought on the Masurian Lakes.

31st Division: Eastern Front, 1915

32nd Brigade: 70 and 174 Regiments
62nd Brigade: 137 and 166 Regiments
                       7. *Ulan* Regiment
31st Artillery Brigade: 31 and 67 Field Artillery
                       Regiments

31st Division was raised in western Germany from Alsace, Lorraine and the Rhineland and was initially part of Sixth Army under Prince Rupprecht. At the beginning of 1915 it was transferred to the Eastern Front joining Hindenburg's army. It took part in the advance from Augustowo in February but was counterattacked by the Russians north of Grodno on 9 March, and during March and April was involved in the battles around Kalwariia and Miriampol. In August it was involved in the offensive upon Vilna, and from October 1915 until 1917 would occupy the Lake Narotch sector. According to American intelligence, 31st Division was 'mediocre' in quality.

8th Division: Loos, 1915

16th Brigade: 72, 93, 153 Regiments
                       10 Hussars (3 squadrons)
8th Artillery Brigade: 74,75 Field Artillery
                       Regiments

Raised in Prussian Saxony, 8th Division originally formed part of von Kluck's First Army during the attack in the west. From June 1915 it was defending the Souchez sector against the French, but three months later during the Battle of Loos it was used in counter attacks and it took heavy casualties. It was a very good division and retained its quality right through to the end of the war.

85th Landwehr Division: Poland, 1915-1916

169th Landwehr Brigade: 61 and 99
                        Landwehr Regiments
170th Landwehr Brigade: 17 and 21
                        Landwehr Regiments
                        85 *Landwehr* cavalry
Artillery: Initially the *Ersatz*
                        detachments of the 36, 71
                        and 73 Field Artillery, later
                        the 85 and 93 Regiments
                        and the 844 Battery.

The 85th *Landwehr* Division, formerly known as the *Breugel* Division, was raised in West Prussia, Alsace and Lorraine. After service on the Western Front it was moved to the East in 1915 seeing action in the Prasnysz sector of Poland. In July it advanced west of Pultusk, besieged Novo-Georgievsk, and then fought on the Bug. 61 Landwehr entered Warsaw in August. Thereafter the Division was employed on the Vichnev sector, south of Krevo, on the Little Berezina. Here it would remain for more than two years. American intelligence rated the formation as 'very mediocre'.

12th Reserve Division: Verdun and the Somme, 1916

22 Reserve Brigade: 23, 38, and 51
                             Reserve Regiments
                             4 Reserve *Ulan* Regiment
12th Reserve Field Artillery (six batteries)

Raised in Silesia, 12th Reserve Division were committed to Verdun in March 1916, taking part in the capture of both Forges and Corbeaux wood, but its efforts against the hill known as the 'Mort Homme' were in vain. Approximately 71% of its infantry strength was lost. Following a very necessary period of rest, 12th Reserve Division was thrown into the Somme, fighting on the Montauban-Hardecourt sector on 2 July. Next it was in the counter attack on Trones wood. As might be expected the Division was enervated for a second time in five months. Perhaps surprisingly American intelligence would continue to rate the 12th Reserve Division as 'second class' very late in the war.

2nd Bavarian Division: Verdun 1916

4th Bavarian Brigade: 12, 15, 20, Bavarian Regiments
                                   4 Bavarian Light Cavalry

2nd Bavarian   2 and 9 Bavarian Field Artillery
Artillery Brigade: Regiments

2nd Bavarian Division was raised in south west Bavaria, and was initially committed to the northern part of the Western Front. In May 1916 it was thrown into the cataclysmic battles around Fort Douaumont in the Verdun sector. It suffered about 50 percent losses. It was later used at Thiaumont and on the Somme during the autumn of 1916. American intelligence rated this division extremely highly.

26th Reserve Division: the Somme July 1916

51st Reserve Brigade: 119 and 180 Reserve Regiments
52nd Reserve Brigade: 121 and 99 Reserve Regiments
                                 Württemburg Reserve Dragoon Regiment
                                 26 Reserve Field Artillery (six batteries)
                                 27 Reserve Field Artillery (six batteries)

This Württemberg division was one of those holding the line on 1 July 1916 when the Franco–British offensive began on the Somme. Its troops occupied Beaumont-Hamel, Ovillers and Thiepval. It was shattered over weeks of hard fighting, but gave as good as it got, until relieved that October. The American assessment was that this was a 'first class' division.

4th Ersatz Division: Belgium and the Somme, 1916

9th *Ersatz* Brigade: 359,360 Regiments
13th *Ersatz* Brigade: 361,362 Regiments
                               4 *Ersatz* cavalry squadron
                               90,91 Field Artillery Regiments

This division was formed in August 1914 by bringing together *Ersatz* battalions from Brandenburg, Schleswig-Holstein, Mecklenburg, the Hanseatic towns and Prussian Saxony. For all of 1915 and the first three months of 1916 it was in the Dixmude sector of Belgium. During October 1916 it served in the Le Sars sector of the Somme. It was rated as a 'fairly good' fighting unit.

101st Division: Serbia and Macedonia, 1916

201st Brigade: 45, 59, and 146 Regiments
                 15 Reserve *Jäger* Battalion
                 11 Dragoon Regiment (2 squadrons)
                 201 Field Artillery Regiment, and
                 Detachment Austro-Hungarian Mountain Artillery (3 batteries)

This division was raised from East Prussia; it served on other parts of the Eastern Front before being deployed against Serbia in 1915. By February 1916, it was at Monastir in Macedonia, and soon afterwards was acting in support of the Bulgarians.

The Alpine Corps: Romania and Italy, 1917

1 Bavarian *Jäger* Brigade: Bavarian *Leib* Regiment;
                                   1 Bavarian *Jäger*; 2 *Jäger*
                                   203 Field Artillery Regiment; and 6 Mountain Artillery detachment

Formed in 1915, the Alpine Corps had served in both France and Italy prior to its deployment to Romania in September 1916. It was in action near Hermannstadt and then Brasso. When the front stabilised it occupied the sector from Panciu to Focsani. A spell of recuperation in Hungary was followed by a brief deployment to the Western Front in the summer of 1917, before it was again committed to the Eastern Front. Autumn 1917 found it fighting on the Izonzo against the Italians. The American estimate of the Alpine Corps was that it was 'an elite body, of genuine combat value' led by crack officers. The fact that it was used both as a specialist unit, and as a 'firefighting' force deployed wherever it was suddenly needed, seem to confirm this opinion.

200th Jäger Division: Carpathians, 1916-1917

2nd *Jäger* Brigade: 3,4,5, *Jäger* Regiments
                            Single squadron of *Ulanen*, originally from the 1 *Ulanen*, later from the 2 *Ulanen*.
                            257 Field Artillery and 7 Mountain Artillery detachment.

The main components of 200th Division, formed in Galicia in July 1916, were three regiments of *Jäger* made up from the pre-existing *Jäger* battalions. These included three battalions of ski troops. During the latter part of 1916 the Division took part in the

Bukovina offensive in the Carpathians against the Russians. It would remain fighting on this front until September 1917 when it would be redeployed to Italy. The Division was recruited from various mountainous parts of Germany including the Harz, Black Forest, and Upper Silesia. The American Intelligence opinion was that this was one of the best divisions 'composed of young vigorous men of high morale'.

16th Bavarian Division: Messines, 1917

9th Bavarian Brigade: 11,14,21 Bavarian Regiments
                          7 Bavarian Light Cavalry
                          (1 squadron)
                          3 Bavarian Field Artillery

This division was formed in January 1917 using regiments from existing divisions. It was moved to the Lys area, near Messines, in June 1917, and was engaged on a number of occasions. In particular it took part in the bloody counter-attack north of the Lys at the end of September and suffered significant losses. The American assessment was that this was a good combat division, which retained high morale despite its losses in the Third Ypres.

11th Division: Passchendaele, 1917

21st Brigade:10 Grenadiers; 38 Füsiliers; 51 Regiment
             2 *Ulan* Regiment (1 squadron)
             42 Field Artillery Regiment

Raised in Silesia, 11th Division was composed mainly of Germans from Breslau, Glatz, and Schweidnitz, and some Poles. The unit saw extensive service in the west including the battle of Arras before taking up its position in the line in Flanders in the summer of 1917. Despite heavy losses it was rated as a very good division; Lieutenant Colonel Schwerk commander of the 51 Infantry was one of the few regimental commanders to win the 'Pour le Mérite'. The quality of the Division had deteriorated only slightly by the end of the war.

17th Division: Picardy, 1918

34th Brigade: 75 Regiment, 89 Grenadiers,
                     90 Füsiliers
                     16 Dragoon Regiment
                     (one squadron)
17 Artillery Command: 60 Field Artillery; detachment
                     24 Foot Artillery (3 batteries)

This division was raised in Schleswig-Holstein, the Hanseatic towns and Mecklenburg, doing extensive service on the Somme and in Belgium, before moving to the Ypres front in July 1917. It was heavily engaged in the Spring offensive of 1918. Between 21 and 25 March it fought south-east of Arras in various engagements during which it lost about 50% of its effectives. It was a division very highly rated both by the Germans and the Allies, winning specific praise from the Kaiser. American Intelligence stated that this and other units of 9th Corps district had officers and men of an 'appreciably higher intellectual level' than average, due to recruitment from the towns of Hamburg, Bremen and Lübeck. There were also some Danes in the ranks, who fought well.

7th Dismounted Cavalry Division: Arras 1918

28th Cavalry Brigade: 11,15 Ulan, 4 Reserve Ulan
30th Cavalry Brigade: 9 Hussar, 15,25, Dragoon
41st Cavalry Brigade: 26 Dragoons, 5 Cuirassier,
                           4 Ulanen
5 Field Artillery (2 batteries)

From the end of August to 9 September 1918, this division was heavily engaged in the Battle of Arras and took heavy losses. The formation of dismounted cavalry divisions was something of an emergency measure in the latter part of the war, and they were never rated as particularly effective. The American assessment of the 7th was as a 'fourth class' unit.

111th Division: Picardy and the Somme, 1918

221st Brigade: 73 *Füsiliers*, 76, 164 Regiments
                22 Dragoons (1 squadron)

111th Artillery 94 Field Artillery and detachment
Command: 25 Foot Artillery (2 batteries)

The 111th Division was raised in the Hanseatic towns and Hanover, and actually formed in 1915. It served extensively on the Western Front prior to its engagement as an assault division in the spring offensive of 1918 when it was in the first wave of the attack. In August and September it held part of the Somme line being heavily assaulted at Favreuil and Hendecourt. American Intelligence opined that it was a good division, used towards the end of the war for 'intervention' in difficult sectors. It showed 'considerable powers of resistance'.

239th Division: Picardy, 1918

239th Brigade: 466,467,468 Regiments
9 Dragoons (1 squadron)
55 Field Artillery, 78 Foot Artillery

Formed from mainly young men of the class of 1918 from Hesse, Hesse-Nassau and Thuringina, this division was deployed first to the Champagne. Following a brief spell in Flanders, the 239th was later committed to the Spring offensive in Picardy, suffering heavily in the attack on Ayette on 27 March. In the latter part of April, the Division was engaged east of Robecq and again lost many casualties. Originally described as a 'fairly good division' and 'better than most' of its type, by October 1918 it was rated by American Intelligence as 'third class' and of low morale.

13th Landwehr Division: St. Mihiel, 1918

60th Landwehr Brigade: 15,60,82 Landwehr
                                          Regiments
                                          6 Dragoons (1 squadron)
                                          13 *Landwehr* Field Artillery

Formed from *Landwehr* regiments from Westphalia, Thuringina and Lorraine the 13th *Landwehr* Division came into existence in 1915 and spent much of the war on the Lorraine front. From the summer of 1918, the Division was in the Combres Les Eparges sector and thus met the American attack on the St Mihiel salient. About 800 men were lost or taken prisoner and the Division was pushed back to Champlon and Marcheville which sector it held at the time of the Armistice. The intelligence assessment was of a 'fourth class' division, 'an inferior sector holding unit of mediocre value'.

ESTABLISHMENTS

Cavalry (1914)

A cavalry division comprised 3 cavalry brigades plus divisional troops; these divisional troops were:

A horse artillery *Abteilung* (3 batteries of 4 guns each);
up to 3 *Jäger* battalions, each with a 6 gun MG
    company;
a mounted MG battery;
pioneer detachment;
heavy and light wireless stations and;
a motor transport column.

Total strength of the cavalry division: at least 5,200 all ranks, 5,600 horses, 12 guns, 12-30 machine guns.

The cavalry brigades were each composed of two regiments, each regiment: 36 officers, 686 other ranks, 765 horses, a telegraph detachment and transport.

The cavalry regiment was of four squadrons, each squadron: 6 officers, 163 other ranks, and 178 horses.

Infantry (1914)

An infantry division comprised two infantry brigades plus divisional troops; these divisional troops were:

a field artillery brigade (72 guns):
a cavalry regiment;
1 or 2 pioneer companies (3 per corps);
a divisional bridging train;
a divisional telephone detachment and
1 or 2 medical companies (3 per corps).

Total strength of the infantry division: 17,500 all ranks, 4,000 horses, 72 guns, 24 machineguns.

The infantry brigades were each composed of two regiments; each regiment: 3 battalions of infantry plus a machinegun company of 6 guns and one spare gun. Total for battalion was 26 officers and 1,050 men. Each infantry battalion was of 4 companies; each company was of 3 platoons totalling 5 officers and 259 men.

A *Jäger* or *Schützen* battalion totalled 4 companies (each of 5 officers and 259 other ranks), an MG company (4 officers and 104 other ranks), and a cyclist company (3 officers and 113 other ranks).

Artillery (1914)

A field artillery brigade was of 2 regiments totalling 72 guns. Each regiment was composed of 2 *Abteilung*, each of 3 batteries and a light ammunition column.

The field artillery battery was 6 guns, 6 ammunition wagons, an observation wagon and transport. Horse batteries were 4 guns and 4 ammunition wagons.

A foot (heavy) artillery regiment of the field army was of two battalions. Each foot artillery battalion was either; 4 batteries of 15 cm howitzers, or 2 batteries of 21 cm mortars. Each battery 4 guns.

Reserve and *Landwehr* (1914)

Reserve Divisions were the same as the active except

that they had 6 field batteries instead of 12. *Landwehr* brigades were 2 regiments of three battalions, 1 squadron and 1 battery.

Machine Gun Units (1914-1918)

The basic machine gun company of 1914 comprised 4 officers and 133 men, with 6 (plus 1 spare), MG 08 machine guns. There were 20 horses and nine wagons (i.e. 6 for the guns, 1 ammunition wagon, 1 supply wagon and 1 field kitchen), there were also 6 small handcarts.

New *Feldmaschinengewehrzüge* and *Maschinengewehr-Ergänzungszüge* (supplementary MG sections) were formed in 1915 and 1916. These were initially often about half the strength of an MG company proper, being later expanded into full blown MG companies, so that by the end of 1916 every infantry battalion had its own 6 gun MG company. Special MG *Scharfschützentrupp*, or 'marksman' sections were also formed with an establishment of 1 officer and 78 other ranks, and these were likewise expanded to full company strength though they acted largely independently of the infantry being deployed as a reserve. Special mountain, cyclist and 8-gun cavalry machine gun squadrons were similarly incorporated. Bergmann light machine gun sections of an officer and 44 men and 9 weapons were formed in 1916 and deployed mainly on the Eastern Front.

Expansion of the MG companies continued during 1917 so that each MG company received a complement of 12 guns. At the same time, light MG 08/15 weapons were issued direct to the infantry on the basis of 3 per company. A typical division would therefore have 108 light and 144 heavy machine guns. In 1918 the issue of light machine guns was increased to 6 per company or 216 per division.

Artillery (1915-1918)

During 1915, field artillery batteries were reduced to four guns or howitzers and many new units were formed, including not only new regiments but a series of independent field batteries in the numbered sequence 801–915 which were used to reinforce the divisional artillery on the Eastern Front. At the end of 1916, the field artillery alone would include 2,100 batteries, but the complement of draught horses was reduced. By April 1916 the establishment of a field artillery battery was:

4 officers
112 other ranks (including 33 gunners and 36 drivers)
101 horses
4 guns or howitzers with limbers
4 ammunition wagons
1 observation wagon
4 other wagons (stores, forage and supply)
1 field kitchen

In 1917, field battery strength was recorded as 6 officers and 130 other ranks and each battery had been issued with a bicycle to further economise on horses.

Mountain gun batteries were introduced after the commencement of hostilities, a *Gebirgskanonen-Batterie* being 4 guns in two sections, with the weapons demountable for pack transport. A 7.5 cm mountain gun formed seven mule loads when dismantled. The establishment of a half battery 'section' at December 1916 was:

2 officers
8 NCOs
59 men
2 7.5 cm mountain guns
31 mules
10 horses

Foot artillery batteries underwent even greater proliferation with the bringing of both new, and obsolete or captured gun types, onto the battlefield. By 1918, the heavy foot artillery batteries were usually arranged with a complement of 2, 3 or 4 guns dependent on type. 13 cm and 15 cm guns were paired; 21 cm mortars were in 3 gun batteries; 10 cm guns and 15 cm howitzers were in 4 gun batteries; obsolete 9 cm guns were grouped into larger batteries of various sizes.

Infantry and close range batteries as used in 1917 and 1918 generally comprised 6 guns, 2 officers, and 60 - 70 other ranks, but were not supplied with horses.

Pioneer Companies (1917)

Pioneers were initially organised in 3 battalion regiments but these were split up to provide handier units to support the field divisions; new regiments were formed for gas and flame thrower duties. By 1917 there were 2 Pioneer field companies per division, their establishment being: 6 officers, 262 other ranks, 20 horses and 7 assorted vehicles. Specialist mining companies were marginally weaker.

Bibliography

Aichner, E., *Deutsche Gebirgstruppen*, Bayerisches Armeemuseum, Ingolstadt, 1983.

Anon, *Die Graue Felduniform der Deutschen Armee*, M. Ruhl Verlag, Leipzig, undated, c. 1914.

Anon, *Die Deutsche Armee: 279 Abbildungen in Farbendruck*, M. Ruhl Verlag, Leipzig, undated, c. 1910.

Anon, *Unser Vaterland in Waffen*, Berlin, undated.

Anon, *Vorschriften Für Kriegsgefangene*, H.M.S.O., 1917.

Anon, *Nachträge und Berichtigung zum Deutschen Reichsheer*, Berlin, 1892.

Baer, Ludwig *The History of the German Steel Helmet*, San Jose, 1985.

Bowman, J.A., *The Pickelhaube*, 2 vols, Lancaster,1989, 1992.

Bruce, Robert, *Machine Guns of World War* I, London, 1997.

Carter, A., *German Bayonets; The Models 98/02 and 98/ 05*, Norwich, 1984

Dean, Bashford *Helmets and Body Armour in Modern Warfare*, New Haven, 1930.

Drury, Ian & Embleton, Gerry, *German Stormtrooper; 1914–1918*, London, 1995.

Ebelshauser, Gustav, A., The *Passage*, Huntington, 1984.

Edkins, D., *The Prussian Order Pour le Mérite*, Falls Church, 1981.

Fisch, Robert, W. *Field Equipment of the Infantry, 1914–1945*. Sykesville, MD, 1989.

Fleischer, W *German Trench Mortars and Infantry Mortars*, Atglen, 1996.

Fosten, D.S.V., *Cuirassiers and Heavy Cavalry Dress Uniforms of the Imperial German Cavalry, 1900–1914*, New Malden, 1973.

Fosten,D.S.V. & Marrion R.J., The *German Army 1914–1918*, London, 1978.

General Staff (British), *Employment of the Minenwerfer*, 1915.

General Staff (British), *Notes on German Army Corps.*

XIV Reserve Corps, and 52nd Division, March, 1916.

General Staff (British).*German Raid on the British Trenches Near La Boiselle*. August, 1916.

General Staff (British), *Summary of Recent Information Regarding the German Army and its Methods*, January, 1917.

General Staff (British), *Information From Captured Documents*, June, 1917.

General Staff (British), *Prisoner of War Companies*, February, 1918.

General Staff (British), *Handbook of the German Army in War*, April, 1918.

General Staff (German), *Instructions Regarding Gas Warfare*, July, 1916.

General Staff (German), *Nahkampfmittel*. [Weapons of Close Combat], Berlin, 1917.

General Staff (U.S.), *Histories of Two Hundred and Fifty-One Divisions of the German Army Which Participated in the War*, Chaumont, France, 1919.

Gudmundsson, Bruce I., *Stormtroop Tactics, Innovation in the German Army, 1914–1918*, New York, 1989.

Goldsmith Dolf, L.*The Devil's Paintbrush*, Toronto, 1989.

Götz, Hans D. *German Military Rifles and Machine Pistols 1871–1945*, 1985, English Edition West Chester, 1990.

Hagger, D.H., *Hussars and Mounted Rifles; Uniforms of the Imperial German Cavalry*, New Malden, 1974.

Hicks, James, E., *German Weapons, Uniform, Insignia, 1841–1918*, La Canada, 1958.

Hormann, Jörg M., *Uniform der Panzertruppe 1917 bis Heute*, Hanau, 1989.

Kaltenegger, Roland, *Die Geschichte der Deutschen Gebirgstruppe 1915 bis Heute*, Stuttgart, 1980.

Kinna, H. & Moss, D.A. .*Jager and Schützen, Dress and Distinctions, 1910–1914*, Watford, 1977.

Kraus, Jürgen, *Stahlhelme*, Bayerisches Armeemuseum, Ingolstadt, 1984.

Kraus, Jürgen, *Vom Bunten Rock Zum Kampfanzug*, Bayerisches Armee Museum, Ingolstadt, 1987.

Haber, Ludwig, F, *The Poisonous Cloud*, Oxford, 1986.

Hamelman, William E., *German Wound Badges*, Dallas, undated.

Hein, Oberleutnant von, *Das Kleine Buch von Deutschen Heere*, Kiel, 1901.

Herwig, Holger H., *The First World War: Germany and Austria Hungary*, London 1997.

Hundleby, M & Strasheim, R., *The German A7V Tank and Captured British Tanks of World War I*, Yeovil, 1990.

Imrie, Alex, *Pictorial History of the German Army Air Service*, Shepperton, 1971.

Jünger, Ernst, *Storm of Steel*, London, 1929.

Jürgens, Hans, *Uniformen des Deutschen Heeres, im Juli 1914: I. Infanterie*, Hamburg, 1954.

Jürgens, Hans, *Uniformen des Deutschen Heeres, im Juli 1914: II. Kavallerie*, Hamburg, 1956.

Knotel, Herbert, *Uniforms of the World*. English Edition, Poole, 1980.

Kube, Jan K., *Militaria der Deutschen Kaizerzeit Helme und Uniformen, 1871–1914*, München, 1977.

Lavisse, E.C., *Field Equipment of the European Foot Soldier*, 1902, reprinted Nashville, 1994.

Military Illustrated, various articles 1986 continuing.

Mollo, Andrew, *Army Uniforms of World War I*, Poole, 1977.

Nash, David, *German Artillery, 1914–1918*, London, 1970.

Nash, David, *German Infantry, 1914–1918*, London, 1971.

Oldham, Peter, *Pill Boxes on the Western Front*, London,1995.

P.P., *Illustrierte Ostdeutsche Kriegs-Zeitung*, 12 vols, Posen 1914–1915.

Paschall, Rod, *The Defeat of Imperial Germany*, Chapel Hill, 1979.

Rankin, Robert, H., *Helmets and Headdress of the Imperial German Army 1870–1918*, New Milford, Connecticut, 1965.

Rhein, Freiherr v. O-S., *Deutschlands Armee in Feldgrauer Kriegs und Friedens-Uniform*, Berlin, 1916.

Rommel, Erwin, *Infantry Attacks*, English Edition, London, 1990.

Samuels, Martin, *Doctrine and Dogma, German and British Infantry Tactics in the First World War*, Westport, Connecticut, 1992.

Senich, P.R., *The German Sniper*. Boulder, Colorado, 1982.

Sigel, G.A.,*Germany's Army and Navy, Chicago*, 1900

Stephens, F.J. & Maddocks, Graham J., *Uniforms and Organisation of the Imperial German Army, 1900–1918*, London, 1975.

Walter, J., *German Military Handguns, London*, 1980.

Walter, J., *The German Rifle, London*, 1979.

Walter, J., *The Luger Book, London*, 1986.

Weiß, Otto, *Feldgrau in Krieg und Frieden*, Berlin 1916–1917: 3 Vols, other ranks; officers and badges.

Wetzig, Sonja, *German Artillery, 1864–1910*, English Edition, Atglen, 1996.

Zienert, J., *Unsere Marineuniform*, Hamburg, 1970.

The cook wagon, or *Küchenwagen*, of fourth battery, *2. Westfälisches Feldartillerie-Regiment Nr 22*, c.1915. Meat is unusually plentiful, but the attitude of the cooks is rather relaxed with their non-regulation pullovers and pets much in evidence. Field artillery regiment Nr 22 served with 13th Division in Belgium at the start of the war, entering France in August 1914. It later fought at Verdun and the Somme.

World War One Directory

Societies and Re-enactment

German First World War re-enactment is in its infancy in the UK, some events of recent years being graced by a solitary figure in a *Pickelhaube*. Perhaps this will change, however, for the *Im Western 1914–1918 Society* has just begun to recreate *Infanterie Regiment Nr 28* in the south-east of England. The point of contact is B. Keene, 9 Wealdon Close, Southwater, Horsham, Sussex, RH13 7HP.

In the United States, Great War German re-enactors are comparatively spoilt for choice. On the West Coast can be found not only a semi-permanent piece of Great War battlefield but two German units, *Garde Grenadier Regiment Nr 1* whose contact is E. Paape, 614 Cayuga Dr., San Jose, CA 95123; and *Infanterie Regiment Nr 63*, this Upper Silesian unit can be contacted via M. Pitt, 3012 Cyprus Rd., Palm Springs, CA. The California area is further catered for by a newsletter, *The Listening Post*, whose contact is P. Carson, 4630 Campus Ave., San Diego, CA 92116.

The East Coast is well provided for. Another contact for *Infanterie Regiment Nr 63* in this area is M. Graef, PO Box 7733, Arlington, VA 22207. Pennsylvania has two units, a *Minenwerfer* company of *Infanterie Regiment Nr 23* contacted care of E. Cowan, Box 552, Chambersburg, PA 1721; and the *Württemburg Infanterie Regiment Nr 120* whose representative is M. Benedict, 1631 Howard Ave., Enola, PA 17025. Not too distant, at least by US standards, are the *Brunswick Nr 92 regiment*, contacted care of R. Brown, 20611 Emerald Dr., Hagerstown, MD 21742, and the *Maschinengewehr Scharfschützen Nr 20*, contact D. Hongell, 25801 Prescott Rd., Clarksburg, MD 20871. The *Bavarian Leib Regiment* in North Carolina can be contacted via K. Allen, PO Box 117, Haw River, NC 25278. New York's *Sturm Pioneer* unit can be reached through J. Michaud, 18 Walnut Ave., Rockville Centre, NY 11570. The American heartland also has at least a trio of interesting units. *Infanterie Regiment Nr 23* can be contacted through R. Zienta, 6416 Gaelic Glen Dr., Oklahoma City, OK 73142: the *Nr 111 Baden* through S. Fisher, 5002 Audrey Circle 203, Indianapolis, IN 46254; and the *Rhineland Landwehr* via G. Giglierano, 1356 Hillcrest Rd, Cincinnati, OH 45224.

Though both the *Western Front Association* research group and the *Great War Society* in the UK concentrate on the Allies, they are both useful starting points for the First World War in general: they may be contacted through R. Clifton, 6 Clarendon Rd, Cambridge, CB2 2BH, and R.G. Carefoot, 18 Risedale Drive, Longridge, Nr Preston, Lancs, PR3 3SB respectively. The *Eastern Front Association* is a new society which may be contacted via the secretary Nik Cornish at Riverside House, Riverside, Chartham, Near Canterbury, Kent CT4 7JT. Martyn Clarke of 165 Marlborough Avenue, Kingston upon Hull, HU5 3LG acts as editor for the *Eastern Front Association* newsletter *Frontovik*.

Books, Wargames and Models

Relatively few books on the Great War German Army are readily available in the English language, and those which are lean heavily on the 1918 *Handbook of the German Army*. The prospective researcher would undoubtedly do well to start by using the bibliography provided in this Brassey's volume, and then use inter-library loan facilities in addition to second-hand book dealers and museum libraries.

Wargamers and modellers are better provided for than was the case even ten years ago. In the UK specialist shops are listed in magazines such as *Miniature Wargames* and *Military Modelling*, and in the pages of Windrow and Greene's *Militaria Directory*. A selection of possible outlets includes *Britannia Miniatures* of 33 St. Mary's Rd., Halton Village, Runcorn, Cheshire, WA7 2JB; *The Guardroom* at 38 West St., Dunstable, Bedfordshire, LU6 ITA; and *IT*

Figures of 193 St. Margaret's Rd., Lowestoft, Suffolk, NR 32 4HN.

Museums and Touring

There are a number of significant public collections of Imperial German Militaria and archives, if one knows where to look. In Germany itself, the premier collections are the Wehrgeschichtliches Museum, Karl Strasse 1, 7550, Rastatt (which includes the Military History Research Office); the Militarhistorisches Museum, Dr Kurt Fisher Platz 3, 8060 Dresden; and the Bayerisches Armeemuseum, Paradeplatz 4 (Neues Schloß), 8070 Ingolstadt, Bayern. In Belgium there is a significant collection of headgear and hardwear at the Musée Royal de l'Armée et d' Histoire Militaire, Parc Du Cinquantenaire 3, Brussels; likewise there is a good deal of captured material at the Musée de l'Armée, Hotel Des Invalides, 75007, Paris, France. In the UK, there is nothing to compare with the Imperial War Museum at Lambeth Rd, London, SE1 6HZ, which has a number of uniforms, small arms, trench mortars and a mass of shoulder straps on display, as well as vital collections which may be consulted by appointment in its reading room and photograph library. Even so, many local regimental collections have something to offer, and a complete list of these may be found in T. Wise *Guide to Military Museums*.

Touring the Western Front is now a well-developed industry. For those travelling under their own steam a copy of Rose Coombes *Before Endeavours Fade* will be a valuable aid. Those who wish to travel from the UK in a group would do well to consult Holt's Tours Ltd, Golden Key Building, 15 Market St., Sandwich, Kent, CT13 9DA, as this company includes not only tours aimed at British subjects and battles but two visits with specific German interest. These are an *Across the Wire Tour* which looks at the German Army and currently includes a lecture and a trip to the site of the Schwaben Redoubt as well as a look at the impressive Langemarck cemetery and the 1918 *Kaiser's Offensive* tour.

Shoulder strap devices of the infantry – worked in red on field grey.

Index

ACKNOWLEDGEMENTS

Many people have given assistance during the production of this book and it is to be hoped that any omitted from the following list will accept my sincere apologies. Firstly I should like to thank Dr Bruce Waller, my former tutor in both German language and history, at University College Swansea, who has since made a considerable mark with his work on Bismarck. At the Imperial War Museum Mike Hibberd, Diana Condell, Hilary Roberts and the staff of the reading room have been especially helpful. John Spencer of the Duke of Wellington's Regiment Museum; Keith Matthews at York Castle Museum; Angela Kelsall at Derby Museum; Simon Jones at National Museums and Galleries on Merseyside; Martin Pegler at the Royal Armouries; and Colonel John Downham and Major Mike Glover of the Queen's Lancashire Regiment have all offered support over and above the call of duty.

Those experts, artists and publishers who have already worked in the field have proved similarly unstinting. These generous people include Martin Windrow, Gerry Embleton, Paul Hannon, John Walter, Anthony Carter, Alan Beadle and Ian Drury. Closer to home another select group have provided support both practical, and moral; they are Tim Newark, Mike Seed, Keith and Penny Edge, and last but certainly not least, Keeley Jones. Thank you all.